Meeting Jesus in the Sacraments

Meeting
JESUS
in the Sacraments

POPE FRANCIS

Our Sunday Visitor Publishing Division
Our Sunday Visitor, Inc.
Huntington, Indiana 46750

20 19 18 17 16 15   1 2 3 4 5 6 7 8 9

ISBN 978-1-61278-831-9 (Inventory No. T1638)
eISBN: 978-1-61278-927-9
LCCN: 2014955294

Cover design: Tyler Ottinger
Cover photo: Stefano Spaziani

PRINTED IN THE UNITED STATES OF AMERICA

TABLE OF CONTENTS

Editor's note: The material in this book is derived from the writings, homilies, and audiences of Pope Francis. The texts have been edited slightly to facilitate presentation in book form. The source of each selection is annotated in attributions after the passage or in footnotes.

Preface[1]

THE SACRAMENTS: CHARISMS AND CHARITY

I have spoken about the Communion of Saints, understood as a communion among holy people, that is among us believers. Now I would like to go in depth into the other aspect of this reality: you will remember that there were two aspects: one is communion, unity, among us, and the other aspect is communion in holy things, *in spiritual goods*. These two aspects are closely connected; in fact, communion among Christians grows through the sharing of spiritual goods. In particular we will consider: *the sacraments, charisms, and charity* (cf. *Catechism of the Catholic Church*, nn. 949–953). We grow in unity, in communion, through: the sacraments, the charisms given to each of us by the Holy Spirit, and charity.

First of all, the *communion of the sacraments*. The sacraments express and realize an effective and profound communion among us, for in them we encounter Christ the Savior and, through him, our brothers and sisters in faith. The sacraments are not mere appearances, they are not rituals; they are the power of Christ; Jesus Christ is present in the sacraments. When we celebrate the Eucharist it is the living Jesus who brings us together, forms us into a community, allows us to adore the Father. Each one of us, in

1   Pope Francis, General Audience, November 6, 2013.

fact, through Baptism, Confirmation, and the Eucharist, is incorporated into Christ and united to the entire community of believers. Therefore, if on the one hand it is the Church that "makes" the sacraments, on the other, it is the sacraments that "make" the Church, that build her up, by generating new children, by gathering them into the holy people of God, by strengthening their membership.

Every encounter with Christ, who in the sacraments gives us salvation, invites us to "go" and communicate to others the salvation that we have been able to see, to touch, to encounter, and to receive, and which is truly credible because it is love. In this way, the sacraments spur us to be missionaries, and the Apostolic commitment to carry the Gospel into every setting, including those most hostile, is the most authentic fruit of an assiduous sacramental life, since it is a participation in the saving initiative of God, who desires salvation for all people. The grace of the sacraments nourishes in us a strong and joyful faith, a faith that knows how to stand in wonder before the "marvels" of God and how to resist the idols of the world. That is why it is important to take Communion, it is important that children be baptized early, that they be confirmed, because the sacraments are the presence of Jesus Christ in us, a presence that helps us. It is important when we feel the weight of our sin to approach the sacrament of Reconciliation. Someone might say: "But I am afraid that the priest will chastise me." No, the priest will not chastise you. Do you know who you will encounter in the sacrament of Reconciliation? You will encounter Jesus, who pardons you! Jesus is waiting for you there; and this is a sacrament that makes the whole Church grow.

A second aspect of communion in holy things is the *communion of charisms*. The Holy Spirit distributes to the faithful a multitude of spiritual gifts and graces; the "imaginative" wealth, let us say, of gifts of the Holy Spirit is ordered to building up the Church. The charisms — that word is a little difficult — are gifts that the Holy Spirit gives us, talents, possibilities…. Gifts given not to be hidden but to be shared with others. They are not given for the benefit of the one who receives them, but for the use of the People of God. If a charism, one of these gifts, serves instead as self-affirmation, then it is doubtful that we are dealing with an authentic charism or one faithfully lived out. The charisms are special graces, given to some for the good of many others. They are attitudes, inspirations, and interior promptings that are born in the consciences and experiences of certain people, who are called to put themselves at the service of the community. In particular, these spiritual gifts further the sanctity of the Church and her mission. We are all called to respect them in ourselves and in others, to receive them as serving the Church's fruitful presence and work. St. Paul warns: "Do not quench the Spirit" (1 Thess 5:19). Let us not quench the Spirit who gives us these gifts, these abilities, these very beautiful virtues that make the Church grow.

What is our attitude to the gifts of the Holy Spirit? Are we aware that the Spirit of God is free to give them to whomsoever he wishes? Do we consider them as a spiritual help, through which the Lord sustains our faith and reinforces our mission in the world?

And we come to the third aspect of communion in holy things, that is, *communion in charity*, the unity among us that creates charity, love. The gentiles, observing the early Christians, said: how they love each other, how they wish one another well! They do not hate, they do not speak against one another. This is the charity, the love of God that the Holy Spirit puts in our hearts. The charisms are important in the life of the Christian community, but they are always a means for growth in charity, in love, which St. Paul sets above the charisms (cf. 1 Cor 13:1–13). Without love, in fact, even the most extraordinary gifts are in vain; this man heals people, he has that power, this other virtue … but does he have love and charity in his heart? If he does then all is well, but if he does not he is no servant of the Church. Without love no gift or charism could serve the Church, for where there is not love there is an emptiness that becomes filled with selfishness. And I ask myself: if we all were egotistical, could we live in communion and peace? No, it's not possible, that is why it is necessary that love unite us. Our smallest gesture of love benefits everyone!

Therefore, to live out unity in the Church and communion in charity means not seeking one's own interests but sharing the suffering and the joy of one's brothers (cf. 1 Cor 12:26), ready to carry the weight of the poorest and the weakest. This fraternal solidarity is not a figure of speech, a saying, but an integral part of the communion among Christians. If we live it, we are a sign to the world, the "sacrament" of God's love. This is what we are one for another and what we are for all! It is not just petty love that we can offer one another, but something much more profound: it is a communion that renders us capable of entering into the joy and sorrow of others and making them sincerely our own.

Often we are too dry, indifferent, and detached and rather than transmitting brotherhood, we communicate bad temper, coldness, and selfishness. And with bad temper, coldness, and selfishness the Church cannot grow; the Church grows only by the love that comes from the Holy Spirit. The Lord invites us to open ourselves to communion with him, in the sacraments, in the charisms, and in charity, in order to live out our Christian vocation with dignity!

Chapter 1[1]

"I Confess One Baptism"

In the *Creed*, through which we make our Profession of Faith every Sunday, we state: "I confess one Baptism for the forgiveness of sins." It is the only explicit reference to a sacrament contained in the *Creed*. Indeed, Baptism is the "door" of faith and of Christian life. The Risen Jesus left the Apostles with this charge: "Go into all the world and preach the Gospel to the whole creation. He who believes and is baptized will be saved" (Mk 16:15–16). The Church's mission is to evangelize and remit sins through the sacrament of Baptism. But let us return to the words of the *Creed*. The expression can be divided into three points: "*I confess*"; "*one Baptism*"; "*for the remission of sins.*"

1. "*I confess.*" What does this mean? It is a solemn term that indicates the great importance of the object, that is, of Baptism. In fact, by pronouncing these words we affirm our true identity as children of God. Baptism is in a certain sense the identity card of the Christian, his birth certificate, and the act of his birth into the Church. All of you know the day on which you were born and you celebrate it as your birthday, don't you? We all celebrate our birthday. I ask you a question that I have already asked several times, but I'll ask it again: who among you remembers the date of your Baptism? Raise your hands: they are few (and I am not

---

asking the Bishops so as not to embarrass them).... Let's do something: today, when you go home, find out what day you were baptized, look for it, because this is your second birthday. The first birthday is the day you came into life and the second birthday is the one on which you came into the Church. Will you do this? This is your homework: find out the day on which you were born to the Church, and give thanks to the Lord, because at Baptism he has opened the door of his Church to us.

At the same time, Baptism is tied to our faith in the remission of sins. The sacrament of Penance, or Confession, is, in fact, like a "second baptism" that refers back always to the first to strengthen and renew it. In this sense, the day of our Baptism is the point of departure for this most beautiful journey, a journey toward God that lasts a lifetime, a journey of conversion that is continually sustained by the sacrament of Penance. Think about this: when we go to confess our weaknesses, our sins, we go to ask the pardon of Jesus, but we also go to renew our Baptism through his forgiveness. And this is beautiful, it is like celebrating the day of Baptism in every Confession. Therefore, Confession is not a matter of sitting down in a torture chamber; rather it is a celebration. Confession is for the baptized! To keep clean the white garment of our Christian dignity!

2. The second element: "*one Baptism.*" This expression refers to that of St. Paul: "one Lord, one faith, one Baptism" (Eph 4:5). The word "Baptism" literally means "immersion," and in fact this sacrament constitutes a true spiritual immersion in the death of Christ, from which one rises with Him like a new creation (cf. Rom 6:4). It is the

washing of regeneration and of illumination. Regeneration because it actuates that birth by water and the Spirit without which no one may enter the Kingdom of Heaven (cf. Jn 3:5). Illumination because through Baptism the human person becomes filled with the grace of Christ, "the true light that enlightens every man" (Jn 1:9) and dispels the shadows of sin. That is why in the ceremony of Baptism the parents are given a lit candle, to signify this illumination; Baptism illuminates us from within with the light of Jesus. In virtue of this gift the baptized are called to become themselves "light" — the light of the faith they have received — for their brothers, especially for those who are in darkness and see no glimmer of light on the horizon of their lives.

We can ask ourselves: is Baptism, for me, a fact of the past, relegated to a date, that date which you are going to go look for today, or is it a living reality that pertains to my present, to every moment? Do you feel strong, with the strength that Christ gave you by his death and his Resurrection? Or do you feel low, without strength? Baptism gives strength, and it gives light. Do you feel enlightened, with that light that comes from Christ? Are you a man or woman of light? Or are you a dark person, without the light of Jesus? We need to take the grace of Baptism, which is a gift, and become a light for all people!

3. Lastly, a brief mention of the third element: *"for the remission of sins."* In the sacrament of Baptism all sins are remitted — original sin and all of our personal sins, as well as the suffering of sin. With Baptism the door to an effectively new life is opened, one that is not burdened by the weight

But already on this earth, in prayer, in the Sacraments, in fraternity, we encounter Jesus and his love, and thus we may already taste something of the risen life. The experience we have of his love and his faithfulness ignites in our hearts like a fire and increases our faith in the resurrection. In fact, if God is faithful and loves, he cannot be thus for only a limited time: faithfulness is eternal; it cannot change. God's love is eternal; it cannot change! It is not only for a time: it is forever! It is for going forward! He is faithful forever and he is waiting for us, each one of us, he accompanies each one of us with his eternal faithfulness.

— *Pope Francis, Angelus, November 10, 2013*

of a negative past, but rather already feels the beauty and the goodness of the Kingdom of Heaven. It is the powerful intervention of God's mercy in our lives, to save us. This saving intervention does not take away our human nature and its weakness — we are all weak and we are all sinners — and it does not take from us our responsibility to ask for forgiveness every time we err! I cannot be baptized many times, but I can go to Confession and by doing so renew the grace of Baptism. It is as though I were being baptized for a second time. The Lord Jesus is very very good and never tires of forgiving us. Even when the door that Baptism opens to us in order to enter the Church is a little closed, due to our weaknesses and our sins. Confession reopens it, precisely because it is a second Baptism that forgives us of everything and illuminates us to go forward with the light of the Lord. Let us go forward in this way, joyfully, because life should be lived with the joy of Jesus Christ; and this is a grace of the Lord.

Chapter 2[1]

Baptism and Forgiveness

In the previous chapter I spoke about the *remission of sins*, referred to in a special way at Baptism. Now let us continue on the theme of the remission of sins, but in reference to the *"power of the keys,"* as it is called, which is a biblical symbol of the mission that Jesus entrusted to the Apostles.

First of all, we must remember that *the principal agent in the forgiveness of sins is the Holy Spirit.* In his first appearance to the Apostles, in the Upper Room, the Risen Jesus made the gesture of breathing on them saying: "Receive the Holy Spirit. If you forgive the sins of any, they are forgiven; if you retain the sins of any, they are retained" (Jn 20:22, 23). Jesus, transfigured in his body, is already the new man who offers the Paschal gifts, the fruit of his death and resurrection. What are these gifts? Peace, joy, the forgiveness of sins, mission, but above all he gives the Spirit who is the source of all these. The breath of Jesus, accompanied by the words with which he communicates the Spirit, signifies the transmission of life, the new life reborn from forgiveness.

But before making this gesture of breathing and transmitting the Holy Spirit, Jesus reveals the wounds in his hands and side: these wounds represent the price of our salvation. The Holy Spirit brings us God's pardon "by pass-

---

1   Pope Francis, General Audience, November 20, 2013.

ing through" Jesus' wounds. These wounds he wished to keep; even now in Heaven he is showing the Father the wounds by which he redeemed us. By the power of these wounds, our sins are pardoned: thus, Jesus gave his life for our peace, for our joy, for the gift of grace in our souls, for the forgiveness of our sins. It is very very beautiful to look at Jesus in this way!

And we come to the second element: Jesus gave the Apostles the power to forgive sins. It is a little difficult to understand how a man can forgive sins, but Jesus gives this power. *The Church is the depository of the power of the keys*, of opening or closing to forgiveness. God forgives every man in his sovereign mercy, but he himself willed that those who belong to Christ and to the Church receive forgiveness by means of the ministers of the community. Through the apostolic ministry the mercy of God reaches me, my faults are forgiven and joy is bestowed on me. In this way Jesus calls us to live out reconciliation in the ecclesial, the community, dimension as well. And this is very beautiful. The Church, who is holy and at the same time in need of penitence, accompanies us on the journey of conversion throughout our lives. The Church is not mistress of the power of the keys, but a servant of the ministry of mercy, and rejoices every time she can offer this divine gift.

Perhaps many do not understand the ecclesial dimension of forgiveness, because individualism, subjectivism, always dominates, and even we Christians are affected by this. Certainly, God forgives every penitent sinner, personally, but the Christian is tied to Christ, and Christ is united to the Church. For us Christians there is a further gift, there is also a further duty: to pass humbly through the ecclesial community. We have to appreciate it; it is a gift, a cure, a protection as well as the assurance that God has forgiven me. I go to my brother priest, and I say: "Father, I did this…." And he responds: "But I forgive you; God forgives you." At that moment, I am sure that God has forgiven me! And this is beautiful, this is having the surety that God forgives us always, he never tires of forgiving us. And we must never tire of going to ask for forgiveness. You may feel ashamed to tell your sins, but as our mothers and our grandmothers used to say, it is better to be red once than yellow a thousand times. We blush once but then our sins are forgiven and we go forward.

Lastly, a final point: *the priest is the instrument for the forgiveness of sins*. God's forgiveness is given to us in the Church, it is transmitted to us by means of the ministry of our brother, the priest; and he too is a man, who, like us in need of mercy, truly becomes the instrument of mercy, bestowing on us the boundless love of God the Father. Priests and bishops too have to go to Confession: we are all sin-

So what is the Church born from? She is born from the supreme act of love of the Cross, from the pierced side of Jesus from which flowed blood and water, a symbol of the sacrament of the Eucharist and of Baptism. The lifeblood of God's family, of the Church, is God's love, which is actualized in loving him and others, all others, without distinction or reservation. The Church is a family in which we love and are loved.

—— *Pope Francis, General Audience, May 29, 2013*

ners. Even the Pope confesses every fifteen days, because the Pope is also a sinner. And the confessor hears what I tell him, he counsels me and forgives me, because we are all in need of this forgiveness. Sometimes you hear someone claiming to confess directly to God.... Yes, as I said before, God is always listening, but in the sacrament of Reconciliation he sends a brother to bestow his pardon, the certainty of forgiveness, in the name of the Church.

The service that the priest assumes a ministry, on behalf of God, to forgive sins is very delicate and requires that his heart be at peace, that the priest have peace in his heart; that he not mistreat the faithful, but that he be gentle, benevolent, and merciful; that he know how to plant hope in hearts and, above all, that he be aware that the brother or sister who approaches the sacrament of Reconciliation seeking forgiveness does so just as many people approached Jesus to be healed. The priest who is not of this disposition of mind had better not administer this sacrament until he has addressed it. The penitent faithful have the right, all faithful have the right, to find in priests servants of the forgiveness of God.

Dear brothers, as members of the Church are we conscious of the beauty of this gift that God himself offers us? Do we feel the joy of this cure, of this motherly attention that the Church has for us? Do we know how to appreciate it with simplicity and diligence? Let us not forget that God never tires of forgiving us; through the ministry of priests he holds us close in a new embrace and regenerates us and allows us to rise again and resume the journey. For this is our life: to rise again continuously and to resume our journey.

Chapter 3[1]

THE SACRAMENTS AND THE
TRANSMISSION OF FAITH

The Church, like every family, passes on to her children the whole store of her memories. But how does this come about in a way that nothing is lost, but rather everything in the patrimony of faith comes to be more deeply understood? It is through the apostolic Tradition preserved in the Church with the assistance of the Holy Spirit that we enjoy a living contact with the foundational memory. What was handed down by the Apostles — as the Second Vatican Council states — "comprises everything that serves to make the people of God live their lives in holiness and increase their faith. In this way the Church, in her doctrine, life, and worship, perpetuates and transmits to every generation all that she herself is, all that she believes" (Second Vatican Ecumenical Council, Dogmatic Constitution on Divine Revelation, *Dei Verbum*, 8).

Faith, in fact, needs a setting in which it can be witnessed to and communicated, a means that is suitable and proportionate to what is communicated. For transmitting a purely doctrinal content, an idea might suffice, or perhaps a book, or the repetition of a spoken message. But what is communicated in the Church, what is handed down in her living Tradition, is the new light born of an encounter with

---

1   Pope Francis, Encyclical Letter, *Lumen Fidei*, June 29, 2013.

the true God, a light which touches us at the core of our being and engages our minds, wills, and emotions, opening us to relationships lived in communion. There is a special means for passing down this fullness, a means capable of engaging the entire person, body and spirit, interior life, and relationships with others. It is the sacraments, celebrated in the Church's liturgy. The sacraments communicate an incarnate memory, linked to the times and places of our lives, linked to all our senses; in them the whole person is engaged as a member of a living subject and part of a network of communitarian relationships. While the sacraments are indeed sacraments of faith (cf. Second Vatican Ecumenical Council, Constitution on the Sacred Liturgy, *Sacrosanctum Concilium*, 59), it can also be said that faith itself possesses a sacramental structure. The awakening of faith is linked to the dawning of a new sacramental sense in our lives as human beings and as Christians, in which visible and material realities are seen to point beyond themselves to the mystery of the eternal.

The transmission of faith occurs first and foremost in baptism. Some might think that baptism is merely a way of symbolizing the confession of faith, a pedagogical tool for those who require images and signs, while in itself ultimately unnecessary. An observation of St. Paul about baptism reminds us that this is not the case. Paul states that "we have been buried with him by baptism into death, so that, just as Christ was raised from the dead by the glory of the Father, we too might walk in newness of life" (Rom 6:4). In baptism we become a new creation and God's adopted children. The Apostle goes on to say that Christians have been entrusted to a "standard of teaching" (*týpos didachés*), which they now obey from the heart (cf. Rom 6:17). In baptism we receive both a teaching to be professed and a specific way of life that demands the engagement of the whole person and sets us on the path to goodness. Those who are baptized are set in a new context, entrusted to a new environment, a new and shared way of acting, in the Church. Baptism makes us see, then, that faith is not the achievement of isolated individuals; it is not an act that someone can perform on his own, but rather something which must be received by entering into the ecclesial communion which transmits God's gift. No one baptizes himself, just as no one comes into the world by himself. Baptism is something we receive.

What are the elements of baptism that introduce us into this new "standard of teaching"? First, the name of the Trinity — the Father, the Son, and the Holy Spirit — is invoked upon the catechumen. Thus, from the outset, a synthesis of the journey of faith is provided. The God who called Abraham and wished to be called his God, the God who revealed his name to Moses, the God who, in giving us his Son, revealed fully the mystery of his Name, now bestows upon the baptized a new filial identity. This is clearly seen in the act of baptism itself: immersion in water. Water is at once a symbol of death, inviting us to pass through self-conversion to a new and greater identity, and a symbol of life, of a womb in which we are reborn by following Christ in his new life. In this way, through immersion in water, baptism speaks to us of the incarnational structure of faith. Christ's work penetrates the depths of our being and transforms us radically, making us adopted children of God

and sharers in the divine nature. It thus modifies all our relationships, our place in this world and in the universe, and
opens them to God's own life of communion. This change
which takes place in baptism helps us to appreciate the singular importance of the catechumenate — whereby growing
numbers of adults, even in societies with ancient Christian
roots, now approach the sacrament of Baptism — for the
new evangelization. It is the road of preparation for baptism,
for the transformation of our whole life in Christ.

To appreciate this link between baptism and faith, we
can recall a text of the prophet Isaiah, which was associ-
ated with baptism in early Christian literature: "Their refuge will be the fortresses of rocks ... their water assured"
(Is 33:16) (cf. *Epistula Barnabae*, 11, 5: SC 172, 162). The
baptized, rescued from the waters of death, were now set
on a "fortress of rock" because they had found a firm and
reliable foundation. The waters of death were thus transformed into waters of life. The Greek text, in speaking of

We must stay ever more deeply connected with Jesus. But
not only that: just as it is important that life blood flow
through the body in order to live, so must we allow Jesus
to work in us, let his Word guide us, his presence in the
Eucharist feed us, give us life, his love strengthen our love
for our neighbor. And this forever! Forever and ever! Dear
brothers and sisters, let us stay united to Jesus, let us trust in
him, let us orient our life according to his Gospel, let us be
nourished by daily prayer, by listening to the Word of God,
by sharing in the Sacraments.

— *Pope Francis, General Audience, June 19, 2013*

that water which is "assured," uses the word *pistós*, "faithful." The waters of baptism are indeed faithful and trustworthy, for they flow with the power of Christ's love, the source of our assurance in the journey of life.

The structure of baptism, its form as a rebirth in which we receive a new name and a new life, helps us to appreciate the meaning and importance of infant baptism. Children are not capable of accepting the faith by a free act, nor are they yet able to profess that faith on their own; therefore the faith is professed by their parents and godparents in their name. Since faith is a reality lived within the community of the Church, part of a common "We," children can be supported by others, their parents and godparents, and welcomed into their faith, which is the faith of the Church; this is symbolized by the candle that the child's father lights from the paschal candle. The structure of baptism, then, demonstrates the critical importance of cooperation between Church and family in passing on the faith. Parents are called, as St. Augustine once said, not only to bring children into the world but also to bring them to God, so that through baptism they can be reborn as children of God and receive the gift of faith. (Cf. *De Nuptiis et Concupiscentia* I, 4, 5: PL 44, 413: *"Habent quippe intentionem generandi regenerandos, ut qui ex eis saeculi filii nascuntur in Dei filios renascantur."*) Thus, along with life, children are given a fundamental orientation and assured of a good future; this orientation will be further strengthened in the sacrament of Confirmation with the seal of the Holy Spirit.

The sacramental character of faith finds its highest expression in the Eucharist. The Eucharist is a precious nourishment for faith: an encounter with Christ truly present in the supreme act of his love, the life-giving gift of himself. In the Eucharist we find the intersection of faith's two dimensions. On the one hand, there is the dimension of history: the Eucharist is an act of remembrance, a making present of the mystery in which the past, as an event of death and resurrection, demonstrates its ability to open up a future, to foreshadow ultimate fulfilment. The liturgy reminds us of this by its repetition of the word *hodie*, the "today" of the mysteries of salvation. On the other hand, we also find the dimension that leads from the visible world to the invisible. In the Eucharist we learn to see the heights and depths of reality. The bread and wine are changed into the body and blood of Christ, who becomes present in his passover to the Father: this movement draws us, body and soul, into the movement of all creation toward its fulfillment in God.

In the celebration of the sacraments, the Church hands down her memory especially through the profession of faith. The creed does not only involve giving one's assent to a body of abstract truths; rather, when it is recited the whole of life is drawn into a journey toward full communion with the living God. We can say that in the creed believers are invited to enter into the mystery that they profess and to be transformed by it. To understand what this means, let us look first at the contents of the creed. It has a trinitarian structure: the Father and the Son are united in the Spirit of love. The believer thus states that the core of all being, the inmost secret of all reality, is the divine communion. The creed also contains a Christological confession: it takes us through all the mysteries of Christ's life up to his death, resurrection, and ascension into heaven before his final return in glory. It tells us that this God of communion, reciprocal love between the Father and the Son in the Spirit, is capable of embracing all of human history and drawing it into the dynamic unity of the Godhead, which has its source and fulfillment in the Father. The believer who professes his or her faith is taken up, as it were, into the truth being professed. He or she cannot truthfully recite the words of the creed without being changed, without becoming part of that history of love which embraces us and expands our being, making it part of a great fellowship, the ultimate subject which recites the creed, namely, the Church. All the truths in which we believe point to the mystery of the new life of faith as a journey of communion with the living God.

Faith, prayer, and the Decalogue

Two other elements are essential in the faithful transmission of the Church's memory. First, the Lord's Prayer, the "Our Father." Here Christians learn to share in Christ's own spiritual experience and to see all things through his eyes. From him who is light from light, the only-begotten Son of the Father, we come to know God and can thus kindle in others the desire to draw near to him.

Similarly important is the link between faith and the Decalogue. Faith, as we have said, takes the form of a journey, a path to be followed, which begins with an encounter with the living God. It is in the light of faith, of complete entrustment to the God who saves, that the Ten Commandments take on their deepest truth, as seen in the words that introduce them: "I am the LORD your God, who brought you out of the land of Egypt" (Ex 20:2). The Decalogue is not a set of negative commands, but concrete directions for emerging from the desert of the selfish and self-enclosed ego in order to enter into dialogue with God, to be embraced by his mercy, and then to bring that mercy to others. Faith thus professes the love of God, origin and upholder of all things, and lets itself be guided by this love in order to journey toward the fullness of communion with God. The Decalogue appears as the path of gratitude, the response of love, made possible because in faith we are receptive to the experience of God's transforming love for us. And this path receives new light from Jesus' teaching in the Sermon on the Mount (cf. Mt 5–7).

These, then, are the four elements that comprise the storehouse of memory the Church hands down: the profession of faith, the celebration of the sacraments, the path of the Ten Commandments, and prayer. The Church's catechesis has traditionally been structured around these four elements; this includes the *Catechism of the Catholic Church,* which is a fundamental aid for that unitary act with which the Church communicates the entire content of her faith: "all that she herself is, all that she believes" (Second Vatican Ecumenical Council, Dogmatic Constitution on Divine Revelation, *Dei Verbum,* 8).

Chapter 4[1]

A Traveling Companion

A sacrament is not "a magical rite" but rather the instrument God has chosen in order to continue to walk beside man as his travelling companion through life. Faced with God's humility, we should have the courage to let him write history, which in that way becomes "reliable." In the history of God's people, there are beautiful moments, which bring great joy, and there are also terrible moments of suffering, martyrdom, and sin. In good and bad moments alike, one thing always remains the same: the Lord is there. He never abandons his people, for the Lord, on that day of sin, of the first sin, made a decision; he made a choice, to make history with his people.

God, who has no history, since he is eternal, wanted to make history, to walk close to his people. But there is more: he wanted to make himself one of us and as one of us to walk with us in Jesus. And this speaks to us. It tells us about the humility of God who is so very great and powerful precisely in his humility.

Walking with God's people, walking with sinners, even walking with the proud: how much the Lord did in order to help the proud hearts of the Pharisees. He wanted

---

1   Pope Francis, Meditation in the Chapel of the Domus St. Martha, September 24, 2013, as reported by *L'Osservatore Romano*, Weekly Edition in English, n. 40, October 2, 2013.

to walk. Humility. God always waits; God is beside us. God walks with us. He is humble. He waits for us always. Jesus always waits for us. This is the humility of God. The Church joyfully sings of the humility of God who accompanies us. The Lord Jesus also accompanies us in our personal lives with the sacraments. A sacrament is not a magical rite, it is an encounter with Jesus Christ. We encounter the Lord. And he is by our side and accompanies us: a traveling companion. The Holy Spirit also accompanies us and teaches us all that we do not know in our hearts. If God entered into our history, let us also enter a little into his history, or at least ask of him the grace to let him write history. May he write our history. It is reliable one.

Chapter 5[1]

THE FOUNDATIONAL SACRAMENT

Baptism is the sacrament on which our very faith is founded and which grafts us as a living member onto Christ and his Church. Together with the Eucharist and Confirmation it forms what is known as "Christian initiation," like one great sacramental event that configures us to the Lord and turns us into a living sign of his presence and of his love.

Yet a question may stir within us: is Baptism really necessary to live as Christians and follow Jesus? After all, isn't it merely a ritual, a formal act of the Church in order to give a name to the little boy or girl? This question can arise. And on this point what the Apostle Paul writes is illuminating: "Do you not know that all of us who have been baptized into Christ Jesus were baptized into his death? We were buried therefore with him by baptism into death, so that as Christ was raised from the dead by the glory of the Father, we too might walk in newness of life" (Rom 6:3–4). Therefore, it is not a formality! It is an act that touches the depths of our existence. A baptized child and an unbaptized child are not the same. A person who is baptized and a person who is not baptized are not the same. We, by Baptism, are immersed in that inexhaustible source of life which is the death of Jesus, the greatest act of love in all of

---

1   Pope Francis, General Audience, January 8, 2014.

history; and thanks to this love we can live a new life, no longer at the mercy of evil, of sin, and of death, but in communion with God and with our brothers and sisters.

Many of us have no memory of the celebration of this sacrament, and it is obvious why, if we were baptized soon after birth. I have asked this question two or three times already, here, in this square: who among you knows the date of your Baptism, raise your hands. It is important to know the day on which I was immersed in that current of Jesus' salvation. And I will allow myself to give you some advice ... but, more than advice, a task for today. Today, at home, go look, ask about the date of your Baptism, and that way you will keep in mind that most beautiful day of Baptism. To know the date of our Baptism is to know a blessed day. The danger of not knowing is that we can lose awareness of what the Lord has done in us, the memory of the gift we have received. Thus, we end up considering it only as an event that took place in the past — and not by our own will but by that of our parents — and that it has no impact on the present. We must reawaken the memory of our Baptism. We are called to live out our Baptism every day as the present reality of our lives. If we manage to follow Jesus and to remain in the Church, despite our limitations and with our weaknesses and our sins, it is precisely in the sacrament whereby we have become new creatures and have been clothed in Christ. It is by the power of Baptism, in fact, that, freed of original sin, we are inserted into Jesus' relation to God the Father; that we are bearers of a new hope, for Baptism gives us this new hope: the hope of going on the path of salvation our whole life long. And this hope nothing and no one can extinguish, for it is a hope that does not disappoint. Remember, hope in the Lord never disappoints. Thanks to Baptism, we are capable of forgiving and of loving even those who offend us and do evil to us. By our Baptism, we recognize in the least and in the poor the face of the Lord who visits us and makes himself close. Baptism helps us to recognize in the face of the needy, the suffering, and also of our neighbor, the face of Jesus. All this is possible thanks to the power of Baptism!

A last point, which is important. I ask you a question: can a person baptize him or herself? No one can be self-baptized! No one. We can ask for it, desire it, but we always need someone else to confer this sacrament in the name of the Lord. For Baptism is a gift which is bestowed in a context of care and fraternal sharing. Throughout history, one baptizes another, another, and another … it is a chain. A chain of Grace. I cannot baptize myself: I must ask another for Baptism. It is an act of brotherhood, an act of filiation to the Church. In the celebration of Baptism we can see the most genuine features of the Church, who like a mother continues to give birth to new children in Christ, in the fecundity of the Holy Spirit.

Let us, then, ask the Lord from our hearts that we may be able to experience ever more, in everyday life, this grace that we have received at Baptism. That in encountering us, our brothers and sisters may encounter true children of God, true brothers and sisters of Jesus Christ, true members of the Church. And do not forget your homework today: find out, ask for the date of your Baptism. As I know my birthday, I should know my Baptism day, because it is a feast day.

Chapter 6[1]

THE FRUIT OF BAPTISM: PEOPLE OF GOD

I would like to stress an important fruit of the sacrament of Baptism: it makes us members of the Body of Christ and of the People of God. St. Thomas Aquinas states that whoever receives Baptism is incorporated in Christ, almost as one of his own limbs, and becomes aggregated to the community of the faithful (cf. *Summa Theologiae*, III, q. 69, art. 5; q. 70, art. 1), that is, the People of God. In the school of the Second Vatican Council, we say today that Baptism allows us *to enter the People of God*, to become members of *a People on a journey*, a people on pilgrimage through history.

In effect, as from generation to generation life is transmitted, so too from generation to generation, through rebirth at the baptismal font, grace is transmitted, and by this grace the Christian People journeys through time, like a river that irrigates the land and spreads God's blessing throughout the world. From the moment that Jesus said what we heard in the Gospel Reading, the disciples went out to baptize; and from that time until today there is a chain in the transmission of the faith through Baptism. And each one of us is a link in that chain: a step forward, always; like a river that irrigates. Such is the grace of God and

---

1   Pope Francis, General Audience, January 15, 2014.

such is our faith, which we must transmit to our sons and daughters, transmit to children, so that once adults, they can do the same for their children. This is what Baptism is. Why? Because Baptism lets us enter this People of God that transmits the faith. This is very important. A People of God that journeys and hands down the faith.

In virtue of Baptism we become *missionary disciples*, called to bring the Gospel to the world (cf. Apostolic Exhortation, *Evangelii Gaudium*, n. 120). "All the baptized, whatever their position in the Church or their level of instruction in the faith, are agents of evangelization.... The new evangelization calls for personal involvement" (ibid.) from everyone, the whole of the People of God, a new kind of personal involvement on the part of each of the baptized. The People of God is *a disciple People* — because it receives the faith — and *a missionary People* — because it transmits the faith. And this is what Baptism works in us: it gives us Grace and hands on the faith to us. All of us in the Church are disciples, and this we are forever, our whole life long; and we are all missionaries, each in the place the Lord has assigned to him or her. Everyone: the littlest one is also a missionary; and the one who seems to be the greatest is a disciple. But one of you might say: "Bishops are not disciples, Bishops know everything; the Pope knows everything, he is not a disciple." No, the Bishops and the Pope must also be disciples, because if they are not disciples, they do no good. They cannot be missionaries; they cannot transmit the faith. We must all be disciples and missionaries.

There exists an indissoluble bond between the *mystical* and the *missionary* dimension of the Christian vocation, both rooted in Baptism. "Upon receiving faith and Baptism, we Christians accept the action of the Holy Spirit who leads to confessing Jesus as Son of God and calling God 'Abba,' Father.... All of us who are baptized ... are called to live and transmit communion with the Trinity, for evangelization is a calling to participate in the communion of the Trinity" (*Final Document of Aparecida*, n. 157).

No one is saved by himself. We are the community of believers, we are the People of God, and in this community we share the beauty of the experience of a love that precedes us all, but that at the same time calls us to be "channels" of grace for one another, despite our limitations and our sins. The communitarian dimension is not just a "frame," an "outline," but an integral part of Christian life, of witness, and of evangelization. The Christian faith is born and lives in the Church, and in Baptism families and parishes celebrate the incorporation of a new member in Christ and in his Body, which is the Church (cf. ibid., n. 175b).

On the subject of the importance of Baptism for the People of God, the history of the *Christian community in Japan* is exemplary. It suffered severe persecution at the start of the seventeenth century. There were many martyrs, members of the clergy were expelled and thousands of faithful killed. No priest was left in Japan; they were all expelled. Then the community retreated into hiding, keeping the faith and prayer in seclusion. And when a child was born, the father or mother baptized him or her, because the faithful can baptize in certain circumstances. When, after roughly two and a half centuries, 250 years later, missionaries returned to Japan, thousands of Christians stepped out into the open and the Church was able to flourish again. They survived by the grace of Baptism! This is profound: the People of God transmits the faith, baptizes her children and goes forward. And they maintained, even in secret, a strong communal spirit, because their Baptism had made of them one single body in Christ: they were isolated and hidden, but they were always members of the People of God, members of the Church. Let us learn a great deal from this history!

Chapter 7[1]

UNITY OF THE BAPTIZED

The *Week of Prayer for Christian Unity* is an invaluable spiritual initiative that has brought Christian communities together for more than a century. It is a time dedicated to prayer for the unity of all the baptized, according to the will of Christ: "that they may all be one" (Jn 17:21). Every year, an ecumenical group from a region of the world, under the guidance of the World Council of Churches and the Pontifical Council for Promoting Christian Unity, suggests the theme and prepares reflections for the *Week of Prayer*. In 2014 it was proposed by the Churches and Ecclesial Communions of Canada, and they made reference to the question St. Paul posed to the Christians of Corinth: "Has Christ been divided?" (1 Cor 1:13).

Of course Christ was not divided. But we should recognize with sincerity and pain that our communities continue to live in division that is scandalous. Division among us Christians is a scandal. There is no other word: a scandal. "Each one of you," St. Paul wrote, "says, 'I belong to Paul,' or 'I belong to Apollos,' or 'I belong to Cephas,' or 'I belong to Christ'" (1:12).

Even those who professed Christ as their leader were not applauded by Paul, because they used the name of Christ to separate themselves from others within the Chris-

---

1   Pope Francis, General Audience, January 22, 2014.

tian community. But the name of Christ creates communion and unity, not division! He came to bring communion among us, not to divide us.

Baptism and the Cross are central elements of the Christian discipleship which we share. Division, however, weakens the credibility and effectiveness of our work in evangelization and risks stripping the Cross of its power (cf. 1 Cor 1:17).

Paul rebukes the Corinthians for their disputes, but he also gives thanks to the Lord "because of the grace of God which was given you in Christ Jesus, that in every way you were enriched in him with all speech and all knowledge" (1 Cor 1:4–5). These words of Paul are not a mere formality, but a sign that he sees primarily — and for this he sincerely rejoices — the gifts given by God to the community. The Apostle's attitude is an encouragement for us and for every Christian community to joyfully recognize God's gifts in other communities. Despite the suffering of divisions, which sadly still exist, let us welcome the words of St. Paul as an invitation to sincerely rejoice for the graces God has given to other Christians. We have the same Baptism, the same Holy Spirit who gave us the Grace: let us recognize it and rejoice in it.

It is beautiful to recognize the grace with which God blesses us and, still more, to find in other Christians something we need, something that we could receive like a gift from our brothers and our sisters. The group from Canada who prepared the texts for the 2014 Week of Prayer did not invite communities to think about what they could give to their neighbor Christians, but urged them to meet with one another in order to understand what they all can receive each from the others. This requires something more. It requires much prayer, it requires humility, it requires reflection and continual conversion. Let us go forward on this path, praying for the unity of Christians, that this scandal lessens and that it may cease among us.

Chapter 8[1]

LIVING OUT OUR BAPTISM

Ash Wednesday marks the beginning of the Lenten journey of forty days, which will lead us to the Easter Triduum, the memorial of the Lord's passion, death, and resurrection and the heart of the mystery of our salvation. Lent prepares us for this most important moment; therefore, it is a "powerful" season, a turning point that can foster change and conversion in each of us. We all need to improve, to change for the better. Lent helps us, and thus we leave behind old habits and the lazy addiction to the evil that deceives and ensnares us. During the season of Lent, the Church issues two important invitations: to have a greater awareness of the redemptive work of Christ; and to live out one's Baptism with deeper commitment.

Awareness of the marvels that the Lord has wrought for our salvation disposes our minds and hearts to an attitude of thanksgiving to God for all that he has given us, for all that he has accomplished for the good of his People and for the whole of humanity. This marks the beginning of our *conversion*: it is the *grateful response to the stupendous mystery of God's love.* When we see the love that God has for us, we feel the desire to draw close to him: this is conversion.

---

1   Pope Francis, General Audience, March 5, 2014.

Living our Baptism to the full — the second invitation — also means *not accustoming ourselves to the situations of degradation and misery* that we encounter as we walk along the streets of our cities and towns. There is a risk of passively accepting certain forms of behavior and of not being shocked by the sad reality surrounding us. We become accustomed to violence, as though it were a predictable part of the daily news. We become accustomed to brothers and sisters sleeping on the streets, who have no roof to shelter them. We become accustomed to refugees seeking freedom and dignity, who are not received as they ought to be. We become accustomed to living in a society that thinks it can do without God, in which parents no longer teach their children to pray or to make the sign of the Cross. I ask you: do your children, do your little ones know how to make the sign of the Cross? Think about it. Do your grandchildren know how to make the sign of the Cross? Have you taught them? Think about it and respond in your heart. Do they know how to pray the "Our Father"? Do they know how to pray to Our Lady with the "Hail Mary"? Think about it and respond within yourselves. Growing accustomed to un-Christian and convenient behavior narcotizes the heart!

Lent comes to us as a providential time to change course, to recover the ability to react to the reality of evil that always challenges us. Lent is to be lived as a time of conversion, as a time of renewal for individuals and communities, by drawing close to God and by trustfully adhering to the Gospel. In this way, it also allows us to look with new eyes at our brothers and sisters and their needs. That is why Lent is a favorable time to convert to the love of God and neighbor; a love that knows how to make its own the Lord's attitude of gratuitousness and mercy — who "became poor, so that by his poverty you might become rich" (2 Cor 8:9). In meditating on the central mysteries of the Faith, the Passion, Cross, and Resurrection of Christ, we shall realize that the immeasurable gift of the Redemption has been granted to us through God's free initiative.

Let us give thanks to God for the mystery of his crucified love; authentic faith, conversion, and openness of heart to the brethren: these are the essential elements for living the season of Lent. On this journey, we want to invoke with special trust the protection and help of the Virgin Mary: may she, who was the first to believe in Christ, accompany us in our days of intense prayer and penance, so that we might come to celebrate, purified and renewed in spirit, the great Paschal mystery of her Son.

Chapter 9[1]

BAPTISM AND EUCHARISTIC COMMUNION

May the power of Christ's Resurrection reach every person — especially those who are suffering — and all the situations most in need of trust and hope.

Christ has fully triumphed over evil once and for all, but it is up to us, to the people of every epoch, to welcome this victory into our lives and into the actual situations of history and society. For this reason it seems to me important to emphasize what we ask God today in the liturgy. "O God, who give constant increase / to your Church by new offspring, / grant that your servants may hold fast in their lives / to the Sacrament they have received in faith" (Collect, Monday within the Octave of Easter).

It is true, yes; Baptism that makes us children of God and the Eucharist that unites us to Christ must become life, that is, they must be expressed in attitudes, behavior, gestures, and decisions. The grace contained in the sacraments of Easter is an enormous potential for the renewal of our personal existence, of family life, of social relations. However, everything passes through the human heart: if I let myself be touched by the grace of the Risen Christ, if I let him change me in that aspect of mine which is not

---

1   Pope Francis, *Regina Caeli*, Easter Monday, April 1, 2013.

good, which can hurt me and others, I allow the victory of Christ to be affirmed in my life, to broaden its beneficial action. This is the power of grace! Without grace we can do nothing. Without grace we can do nothing! And with the grace of Baptism and of Eucharistic Communion I can become an instrument of God's mercy, of that beautiful mercy of God.

To express in life the sacrament we have received: dear brothers and sisters, this is our daily duty, but I would also say our daily joy! The joy of feeling we are instruments of Christ's grace, like branches of the vine that is Christ himself, brought to life by the sap of his Spirit!

Let us pray together, in the name of the dead and Risen Lord and through the intercession of Mary Most Holy, that the Paschal Mystery may work profoundly within us and in our time so that hatred may give way to love, falsehood to truth, revenge to forgiveness, and sadness to joy.

Chapter 10[1]

MAKING BAPTISMAL FAITH OUR OWN

What inspired Paul's passion? It was the fire of love with which Christ shed his blood in his own Passion, and the desire he has to recreate us in his blood. "What Christ accomplished in us is a recreation. The blood of Christ has recreated us; it is a second creation. And if, before, our lives, our bodies, our souls, and our habits followed the way of sin and iniquity, after this recreation, we must make every effort to walk along the way of justice and sanctification."

When we were baptized, our parents made the act of faith on our behalf: I believe in Jesus Christ who has forgiven our sins. We must make this faith our own and carry it forward by our way of life. And living as a Christian means carrying forward this faith in Christ, this recreation. Carrying forward the works that are born of faith.... Here we are then: the first sanctification accomplished by Christ, the first sanctification we received in baptism, must grow; it must advance.

Yet we are weak, and we often fall. Does this mean that we are not on the road of sanctification? Yes and no.... If you grow accustomed to a life that is mediocre, and you

---

1   Pope Francis, Meditation in the Chapel of the Domus St. Martha, October 24, 2013, as reported by *L'Osservatore Romano*, Weekly Edition in English, n. 44, November 1, 2013.

say, "I believe in Jesus Christ, but I live as I want," then this does not sanctify you, it is not all right, it is absurd. But if you say, "Yes, I am a sinner; I am weak," and you continually turn to the Lord and say to him: "Lord, you have the power, increase my faith; you can heal me," then through the sacrament of Reconciliation even our imperfections are taken up into this way of sanctification.

Leaving everything behind for Christ was Paul's passion, and it should be the passion of every Christian: to suffer the loss of everything that draws us away from Christ, the Lord; to suffer the loss of all that draws us away from our act of faith in him, from our act of faith in the recreation he has accomplished by his blood. He makes all things new. Everything is made new in Christ. Everything is new.

Chapter 11[1]

BAPTIZING CHILDREN —
AN UNINTERRUPTED CHAIN

Jesus did not need to be baptized, but the first theologians say that, with his body, with his divinity, in baptism he blessed all the waters, so that the waters would have the power to confer baptism. And then, before ascending to Heaven, Jesus told us to go into all the world to baptize. And from that day forward up until today, this has been an uninterrupted chain: they baptized their children, and their children their own, and those children.... And also today this chain continues.

These children are a link in a chain. You parents have a baby boy or girl to baptize, but in some years they will have a child to baptize, or a grandchild.... Such is the chain of faith! What does this mean? I would like to tell you only this: you are those who transmit the faith, the transmitters; you have a duty to hand on the faith to these children. It is the most beautiful inheritance you will leave to them: the faith! Only this. Today, take this thought home with you. We must be transmitters of the faith. Think about this, always think about how to hand on the faith to your children.

---

1   Pope Francis, Homily, Feast of the Baptism of the Lord, January 12, 2014.

Today the choir sings, but the most beautiful choir is the children making noise.... Some of them will cry, because they are uncomfortable or because they are hungry: if they are hungry, mothers, feed them with ease, because they are the most important ones here. And now, with this awareness of being transmitters of the faith, let us continue with the rite of Baptism.

Chapter 12[1]

CHILDREN OF GOD

I would like to reflect on the saving capacity of the Resurrection of Jesus. What does the Resurrection mean for our life? And why is our faith in vain without it?

Our faith is founded on Christ's death and Resurrection, just as a house stands on its foundations: if they give way, the whole house collapses. Jesus gave himself on the Cross, taking the burden of our sins upon himself and descending into the abyss of death, then in the Resurrection he triumphed over them, took them away and opened before us the path to rebirth and to a new life.

St. Peter summed this up at the beginning of his First Letter: "Blessed be the God and Father of our Lord Jesus Christ! By his great mercy we have been born anew to a living hope through the Resurrection of Jesus Christ from the dead, and to an inheritance which is imperishable, undefiled, and unfading" (1 Pet 1:3–4).

The Apostle tells us that with the Resurrection of Jesus something absolutely new happens: we are set free from the slavery of sin and become children of God; that is, we are born to new life. When is this accomplished for us? In the sacrament of Baptism. In ancient times, it was customarily received through immersion. The person who was to be baptized walked down into the great basin of the Baptis-

---

1   Pope Francis, General Audience, April 10, 2013.

tery, stepping out of his clothes, and the Bishop or Priest poured water on his head three times, baptizing him in the name of the Father, of the Son, and of the Holy Spirit. Then the baptized person emerged from the basin and put on a new robe, the white one; in other words, by immersing himself in the death and Resurrection of Christ he was born to new life. He had become a son of God. In his Letter to the Romans, St. Paul wrote: "You have received the spirit of sonship, When we cry 'Abba! Father!' it is the Spirit himself bearing witness with our spirit that we are children of God" (Rom 8:15–16).

It is the Spirit himself whom we received in Baptism who teaches us, who spurs us to say to God: "Father" or, rather, "Abba!" which means "papa" or "dad." Our God is like this: he is a dad to us. The Holy Spirit creates within us this new condition as children of God. And this is the greatest gift we have received from the Paschal Mystery of Jesus. Moreover, God treats us as children, he understands us, he forgives us, he embraces us, he loves us even when we err. In the Old Testament, the Prophet Isaiah was already affirming that even if a mother could forget her child, God never forgets us at any moment (cf. 49:15). And this is beautiful!

Yet this filial relationship with God is not like a treasure that we keep in a corner of our life, but must be increased. It must be nourished every day with listening to the word of God, with prayer, with participation in the sacraments, especially Reconciliation and the Eucharist, and with love. We can live as children! And this is our dignity — we have the dignity of children. We should behave as true children! This means that every day we must let Christ transform us and conform us to him; it means striving to live as Christians, endeavoring to follow him in spite of seeing our limitations and weaknesses. The temptation to set God aside in order to put ourselves at the center is always at the door, and the experience of sin injures our Christian life, our being children of God. For this reason we must have the courage of faith not to allow ourselves to be guided by the mentality that tells us: "God is not necessary, he is not important for you," and so forth. It is exactly the opposite: only by behaving as children of God, without despairing at our shortcomings, at our sins, only by feeling loved by him will our life be new, enlivened by serenity and joy. God is our strength! God is our hope!

We must be the first to have this steadfast hope, and we must be a visible, clear, and radiant sign of it for everyone. The Risen Lord is the hope that never fails, that never disappoints (cf. Rom 5:5). Hope does not let us down — the hope of the Lord! How often in our life do hopes vanish; how often do the expectations we have in our heart come to nothing! Our hope as Christians is strong, safe and sound on this earth, where God has called us to walk, and it is open to eternity because it is founded on God who is always faithful. We must not forget: God is always faithful to us. Being raised with Christ through Baptism, with the gift of faith, an inheritance that is incorruptible, prompts us to seek God's things more often, to think of him more often and to pray to him more.

Being Christian is not just obeying orders, but means being in Christ, thinking like him, acting like him, loving like him; it means letting him take possession of our life and change it, transform it, and free it from the darkness of evil and sin.

Let us point out the Risen Christ to those who ask us to account for the hope that is in us (cf. 1 Pet 3:15). Let us point him out with the proclamation of the word, but above all with our lives as people who have been raised. Let us show the joy of being children of God, the freedom that living in Christ gives us, which is true freedom, the freedom that saves us from the slavery of evil, of sin, and of death! Looking at the heavenly homeland, we shall receive new light and fresh strength, both in our commitment and in our daily efforts.

This is a precious service, which we must give to this world of ours that all too often no longer succeeds in raising its gaze on high, no longer succeeds in raising its gaze to God.

Chapter 13[1]

THE CHURCH BORN FROM LOVE

When we read the Gospels, we see that Jesus gathers around him a small community that receives his word, follows it, shares in his journey, becomes his family; and it is with this community that he prepares and builds his Church.

So what is the Church born from? She is born from the supreme act of love of the Cross, from the pierced side of Jesus from which flowed blood and water, a symbol of the sacrament of the Eucharist and of Baptism. The life-blood of God's family, of the Church, is God's love, which is actualized in loving him and others, all others, without distinction or reservation. The Church is a family in which we love and are loved.

When did the Church manifest herself? We celebrated it two Sundays ago; she became manifest when the gift of the Holy Spirit filled the heart of the Apostles and spurred them to go out and begin their journey to proclaim the Gospel, spreading God's love.

Still today some say, "Christ yes, the Church no." Like those who say, "I believe in God but not in priests." But it is the Church herself which brings Christ to us and which brings us to God. The Church is the great family of God's children. Of course, she also has human aspects. In those

---

1   Pope Francis, General Audience, May 29, 2013.

who make up the Church, pastors and faithful, there are shortcomings, imperfections, and sins. The Pope has these too — and many of them; but what is beautiful is that when we realize we are sinners we encounter the mercy of God who always forgives. Never forget it: God always pardons and receives us into his love of forgiveness and mercy. Some people say that sin is an offense to God, but also an opportunity to humble oneself so as to realize that there is something else more beautiful: God's mercy. Let us think about this.

Chapter 14[1]

CHRISTIAN INITIATION

Continuing our catechesis on the sacraments, we pause to reflect on Confirmation, or "Chrismation," which must be understood in continuity with Baptism, to which it is inseparably linked. These two sacraments, together with the Eucharist, form a single saving event — called "Christian initiation" — in which we are inserted into Jesus Christ, who died and rose, and become new creatures and members of the Church. This is why these three sacraments were originally celebrated on one occasion, at the end of the catechumenal journey, normally at the Easter Vigil. The path of formation and gradual insertion into the Christian community, which could last even up to a few years, was thus sealed. One travelled step by step to reach Baptism, then Confirmation and the Eucharist.

We commonly speak of the sacrament of "Chrismation," a word that signifies "anointing." And, in effect, through the oil called "sacred Chrism," we are conformed, in the power of the Spirit, to Jesus Christ, who is the only true "anointed One," the "Messiah," the Holy One of God. The word "Confirmation" then reminds us that this sacrament brings an increase and deepening of baptismal grace: it unites us more firmly to Christ, it renders our bond with

---

1   Pope Francis, General Audience, January 21, 2014.

the Church more perfect, and it gives us a special strength of the Holy Spirit to spread and defend the faith,… to confess the name of Christ boldly, and never to be ashamed of his Cross (cf. *Catechism of the Catholic Church*, n. 1303).

For this reason, it is important to take care that our children, our young people, receive this sacrament. We all take care that they are baptized and this is good, but perhaps we do not take so much care to ensure that they are confirmed. Thus they remain at a midpoint in their journey and do not receive the Holy Spirit, who is so important in the Christian life since he gives us the strength to go on. Let us think a little, each one of us: do we truly care whether our children, our young people, receive Confirmation? This is important; it is important! And if you have children or adolescents at home who have not yet received it and are at the age to do so, do everything possible to ensure that they complete their Christian initiation and receive the power of the Holy Spirit. It is important!

Naturally, it is important to prepare those being confirmed well, leading them toward a personal commitment to faith in Christ and reawakening in them a sense of belonging to the Church.

Confirmation, like every sacrament, is not the work of men but of God, who cares for our lives in such a manner as to mold us in the image of his Son, to make us capable of loving like him. He does it by infusing in us his Holy Spirit, whose action pervades the whole person and his entire life, as reflected in the seven gifts that Tradition, in light of the Sacred Scripture, has always highlighted. These seven gifts: I do not want to ask you if you remember the seven gifts.

Perhaps you will all know them.... But I will say them on your behalf. What are these gifts? Wisdom, Understanding, Counsel, Fortitude, Knowledge, Piety, and Fear of the Lord. And these gifts have been given to us precisely with the Holy Spirit in the sacrament of Confirmation. When we welcome the Holy Spirit into our hearts and allow him to act, Christ makes himself present in us and takes shape in our lives; through us, it will be he — Christ himself — who prays, forgives, gives hope and consolation, serves the brethren, draws close to the needy and to the least, creates community, and sows peace. Think how important this is: by means of the Holy Spirit, Christ himself comes to do all this among us and for us. That is why it is important that children and young people receive the sacrament of Confirmation.

Now, this is a good question: who is the driving force of the Church's unity? It is the Holy Spirit, whom we have all received at Baptism and also in the Sacrament of Confirmation. It is the Holy Spirit. Our unity is not primarily a fruit of our own consensus or of the democracy in the Church, or of our effort to get along with each other; rather, it comes from the One who creates unity in diversity, because the Holy Spirit is harmony and always creates harmony in the Church. And harmonious unity in the many different cultures, languages, and ways of thinking. The Holy Spirit is the mover. This is why prayer is important. It is the soul of our commitment as men and women of communion, of unity. Pray to the Holy Spirit that he may come and create unity in the Church.

— *Pope Francis, General Audience, September 25, 2013*

Dear brothers and sisters, let us remember that we have received Confirmation! All of us! Let us remember it, first in order to thank the Lord for this gift, and then to ask him to help us to live as true Christians, to walk always with joy in the Holy Spirit who has been given to us.

Chapter 15[1]

Confirmation and Steadfastness

I would like to offer three short and simple thoughts for your reflection.

1. In the second reading, we listened to the beautiful vision of St. John: new heavens and a new earth, and then the Holy City coming down from God. All is new, changed into good, beauty, and truth; there are no more tears or mourning.... This is the work of the Holy Spirit: he brings us the new things of God. He comes to us and makes all things new; he changes us. The Spirit changes us! And St. John's vision reminds us that all of us are journeying toward the heavenly Jerusalem, the ultimate newness which awaits us and all reality, the happy day when we will see the Lord's face — that marvelous face, the most beautiful face of the Lord Jesus — and be with him forever, in his love.

You see, the new things of God are not like the novelties of this world, all of which are temporary; they come and go, and we keep looking for more. The new things that God gives to our lives are lasting, not only in the future, when we will be with him, but today as well. God is even now making all things new; the Holy Spirit is truly transforming us, and through us he also wants to transform the world in which we live. Let us open the doors to the Spirit, let ourselves be guided by him, and allow God's constant

---

1   Pope Francis, Homily, April 28, 2013.

help to make us new men and women, inspired by the love of God which the Holy Spirit bestows on us! How beautiful it would be if each of you, every evening, could say: Today at school, at home, at work, guided by God, I showed a sign of love toward one of my friends, my parents, an older person! How beautiful!

2. A second thought. In the first reading, Paul and Barnabas say that we must undergo many trials if we are to enter the kingdom of God (cf. Acts 14:22). The journey of the Church and our own personal journeys as Christians are not always easy; they meet with difficulties and trials. To follow the Lord, to let his Spirit transform the shadowy parts of our lives, our ungodly ways of acting, and cleanse us of our sins, is to set out on a path with many obstacles, both in the world around us but also within us, in the heart. But difficulties and trials are part of the path that leads to God's glory, just as they were for Jesus, who was glorified on the cross; we will always encounter them in life! Do not be discouraged! We have the power of the Holy Spirit to overcome these trials!

Dear brothers and sisters, we need to let ourselves be bathed in the light of the Holy Spirit so that he may lead us into the Truth of God, who is the one Lord of our life. In this Year of Faith let us ask ourselves whether we really have taken some steps to know Christ and the truth of faith better by reading and meditating on Sacred Scripture, by studying the *Catechism*, and by receiving the sacraments regularly.

— *Pope Francis, General Audience, May 15, 2013*

3. And here I come to my last point. It is an invitation that I make to you, young confirmandi, and to all present. Remain steadfast in the journey of faith, with firm hope in the Lord. This is the secret of our journey! He gives us the courage to swim against the tide. Pay attention, my young friends: to go against the current; this is good for the heart, but we need courage to swim against the tide. Jesus gives us this courage! There are no difficulties, trials, or misunderstandings to fear, provided we remain united to God as branches to the vine, provided we do not lose our friendship with him, provided we make ever more room for him in our lives. This is especially so whenever we feel poor, weak, and sinful, because God grants strength to our weakness, riches to our poverty, conversion and forgiveness to our sinfulness. The Lord is so rich in mercy: every time, if we go to him, he forgives us. Let us trust in God's work! With him we can do great things; he will give us the joy of being his disciples, his witnesses. Commit yourselves to great ideals, to the most important things. We Christians were not chosen by the Lord for little things; push onwards toward the highest principles. Stake your lives on noble ideals, my dear young people!

The new things of God, the trials of life, remaining steadfast in the Lord. Dear friends, let us open wide the door of our lives to the new things of God that the Holy Spirit gives us. May he transform us, confirm us in our trials, strengthen our union with the Lord, our steadfastness in him: this is a true joy! So may it be.

Chapter 16[1]

THE EUCHARIST, THE SACRAMENT OF LOVE

In this chapter, I will speak about the Eucharist. The Eucharist is at the heart of "Christian initiation," together with Baptism and Confirmation, and it constitutes the source of the Church's life itself. From this sacrament of love, in fact, flows every authentic journey of faith, of communion, and of witness.

What we see when we gather to celebrate the Eucharist, the Mass, already gives us an intuition of what we are about to live. At the center of the space intended for the celebration there is an altar, which is a table covered with a tablecloth, and this makes us think of a banquet. On the table there is a cross to indicate that on this altar what is offered is the sacrifice of Christ: he is the spiritual food that we receive there, under the species of bread and wine. Beside the table is the ambo, the place from which the Word of God is proclaimed: and this indicates that there we gather to listen to the Lord who speaks through Sacred Scripture, and therefore the food that we receive is also his Word.

Word and Bread in the Mass become one, as at the Last Supper, when all the words of Jesus, all the signs that he had performed, were condensed into the gesture of

---

1 Pope Francis, General Audience, February 5, 2014.

breaking the bread and offering the chalice, in anticipation
of the sacrifice of the cross, and in these words: "Take, eat;
this is my body.... Take, drink of it; for this is my blood."

Jesus' gesture at the Last Supper is the ultimate thanksgiving to the Father for his love, for his mercy. "Thanksgiving" in Greek is expressed as "eucharist." And that is why
the sacrament is called the Eucharist: it is the supreme
thanksgiving to the Father, who so loved us that he gave us
his Son out of love. This is why the term Eucharist includes
the whole of that act, which is the act of God and man
together, the act of Jesus Christ, true God and true Man.

Therefore the Eucharistic Celebration is much more
than a simple banquet: it is exactly the memorial of Jesus' Paschal Sacrifice, the mystery at the center of salvation.
"Memorial" does not simply mean a remembrance, a mere
memory; it means that every time we celebrate this sacrament we participate in the mystery of the passion, death,
and resurrection of Christ. The Eucharist is the summit of
God's saving action: the Lord Jesus, by becoming bread
broken for us, pours upon us all of his mercy and his love,
so as to renew our hearts, our lives, and our way of relating
with him and with the brethren. It is for this reason that
commonly, when we approach this sacrament, we speak
of "receiving Communion," of "taking Communion": this
means that, by the power of the Holy Spirit, participation
in Holy Communion conforms us in a singular and profound way to Christ, giving us a foretaste already now of
the full communion with the Father that characterizes the
heavenly banquet, where together with all the Saints we
will have the joy of contemplating God face to face.

St. Ignatius of Antioch has that essential expression with which he defines the Church of Rome: "the Church which presides in charity" (*Letter to the Romans*, greeting). I therefore ask you to cooperate "in faith and in the charity of Jesus Christ our Lord" (ibid.), reminding you that our action will only be effective if it is rooted in faith and nourished by prayer, especially by the Blessed Eucharist, the Sacrament of faith and charity.

—— *Pope Francis, Address to Assembly of Organization for Aid to the Eastern Churches, June 20, 2013*

Dear friends, we don't ever thank the Lord enough for the gift he has given us in the Eucharist! It is a very great gift, and that is why it is so important to go to Mass on Sunday. Go to Mass not just to pray, but to receive Communion, the bread that is the Body of Jesus Christ who saves us, forgives us, unites us to the Father. It is a beautiful thing to do! And we go to Mass every Sunday because that is the day of the resurrection of the Lord. That is why Sunday is so important to us. And in this Eucharist we feel this belonging to the Church, to the People of God, to the Body of God, to Jesus Christ. We will never completely grasp the value and the richness of it. Let us ask him then that this sacrament continue to keep his presence alive in the Church and to shape our community in charity and communion, according to the Father's heart. This is done throughout life, but is begun on the day of our First Communion. It is important that children be prepared well for their First Communion and that every child receive it, because it is the first step of this intense belonging to Jesus Christ, after Baptism and Confirmation.

Chapter 17[1]

EUCHARIST AND LIFE

In the last chapter, I emphasized how the Eucharist introduces us into real communion with Jesus and his mystery. Now let us ask ourselves several questions that spring from the relationship between the Eucharist that we celebrate and our life, as a Church and as individual Christians. *How do we experience the Eucharist?* When we go to Sunday Mass, how do we live it? Is it only a moment of celebration, an established tradition, an opportunity to find oneself or to feel justified, or is it something more?

There are very specific signals for understanding how we are living this, how we experience the Eucharist; signals that tell us if we are living the Eucharist in a good way or not very well. The first indicator is our *way of looking at or considering others*. In the Eucharist, Christ is always renewing his gift of self, which he made on the Cross. His whole life is an act of total sharing of self out of love; thus, he loved to be with his disciples and with the people whom he had a chance to know. This meant for him sharing in their aspirations, their problems, what stirred their soul and their life. Now we — when participating in Holy Mass — we find ourselves with all sorts of men and women: young people, the elderly, children; poor and well off; locals and strangers alike; people with their families and people who

---

1 Pope Francis, General Audience, February 12, 2014.

75

are alone.... But the Eucharist that I celebrate, does it lead me to truly feel they are all like brothers and sisters? Does it increase my capacity to rejoice with those who are rejoicing and cry with those who are crying? Does it urge me to go out to the poor, the sick, the marginalized? Does it help me to recognize in others the face of Jesus?

We all go to Mass because we love Jesus and we want to share, through the Eucharist, in his passion and his resurrection. But do we love, as Jesus wishes, those brothers and sisters who are the most needy? For example, in Rome these days we have seen much social discomfort either due to the rain, which has caused so much damage to entire districts, or because of the lack of work, a consequence of the global economic crisis. I wonder, and each one of us should wonder: I who go to Mass, how do I live this? Do I try to help, to approach and pray for those in difficulty? Or am I a little indifferent? Or perhaps do I just want to talk: did you see how this or that one is dressed? Sometimes this happens after Mass and it should not! We must concern ourselves with our brothers and sisters who need us because of an illness, a problem. Today, it would do us such good to think of these brothers and sisters of ours who are beset by these problems here in Rome: problems that stem from the grave situation caused by the rain and social instability and unemployment. Let us ask Jesus, whom we receive in the Eucharist, to help us to help them.

A second indication, a very important one, is the grace of *feeling forgiven and ready to forgive*. At times someone may ask: "Why must one go to Church, given that those who regularly participate in Holy Mass are still sinners like the others?" We have heard it many times! In reality, the one celebrating the Eucharist doesn't do so because he believes he is or wants to appear better than others, but precisely because he acknowledges that he is always in need of being accepted and reborn by the mercy of God made flesh in Jesus Christ. If any one of us does not feel in need of the mercy of God, does not see himself as a sinner, it is better for him not to go to Mass! We go to Mass because we are sinners and we want to receive God's pardon, to participate in the redemption of Jesus, in his forgiveness. The "Confession" which we make at the beginning is not "pro forma," it is a real act of repentance! I am a sinner and I confess it, this is how the Mass begins! We should never forget that the Last Supper of Jesus took place "on the night he was betrayed" (1 Cor 11:23). In the bread and in the wine that we offer and around which we gather, the gift of Christ's body and blood is renewed every time for the remission of our sins. We must go to Mass humbly, like sinners, and the Lord reconciles us.

A last valuable indication comes to us from the relationship between the Eucharistic Celebration and *the life of our Christian communities*. We must always bear in mind that the Eucharist is not something we make; it is not our own commemoration of what Jesus said and did. No. It is precisely an act of Christ! It is Christ who acts there, who is on the altar. It is a gift of Christ, who makes himself present and gathers us around him, to nourish us with his Word and with his life. This means that the mission and the very identity of the Church flows from there, from the Eucharist, and there always takes its shape. A celebration may be flawless on the exterior, very beautiful, but if it does not lead us to encounter Jesus Christ, it is unlikely to bear any kind of nourishment to our heart and our life. Through the Eucharist, however, Christ wishes to enter into our life and permeate it with his grace, so that in every Christian community there may be coherence between liturgy and life.

The heart fills with trust and hope by pondering on Jesus' words recounted in the Gospel: "He who eats my flesh and drinks my blood has eternal life, and I will raise him up at the last day" (Jn 6:54). Let us live the Eucharist with the spirit of faith, of prayer, of forgiveness, of repentance, of communal joy, of concern for the needy and for the needs of so many brothers and sisters, in the certainty that the Lord will fulfill what he has promised us: eternal life. So be it!

Chapter 18[1]

GOD'S MERCY IN CONFESSION

Through the sacraments of Christian Initiation —
Baptism, Confirmation, and the Eucharist — man
receives new life in Christ. Now we all know that
we carry this life "in earthen vessels" (2 Cor 4:7), we are still
subject to temptation, suffering, and death, and, because of
sin, we may even lose this new life. That is why the Lord
Jesus willed that the Church continue his saving work even
to her own members, especially through the sacraments of
Reconciliation and the Anointing of the Sick, which can
be united under the heading of "sacraments of Healing."
The sacrament of Reconciliation is a sacrament of healing.
When I go to Confession, it is in order to be healed, to heal
my soul, to heal my heart and to be healed of some wrong-
doing. The biblical icon which best expresses them in their
deep bond is the episode of the forgiving and healing of the
paralytic, where the Lord Jesus is revealed at the same time
as the physician of souls and of bodies (cf. Mk 2:1–12; Mt
9:1–8; Lk 5:17–26).

The sacrament of Penance and Reconciliation flows
directly from the Paschal Mystery. In fact, on the evening
of Easter the Lord appeared to the disciples, who were
locked in the Upper Room, and after addressing them with
the greeting, "Peace be with you!" he breathed on them and

---

1   Pope Francis, General Audience, February 19, 2014.

said: "Receive the Holy Spirit. If you forgive the sins of any, they are forgiven" (Jn 20:21–23). This passage reveals to us the most profound dynamic contained in this sacrament.

First, the fact that the forgiveness of our sins is not something we can give ourselves. I cannot say: I forgive my sins. Forgiveness is asked for, is asked of another, and in Confession we ask for forgiveness from Jesus. Forgiveness is not the fruit of our own efforts but rather a gift, it is a gift of the Holy Spirit who fills us with the wellspring of mercy and of grace that flows unceasingly from the open heart of the Crucified and Risen Christ. Secondly, it reminds us that we can truly be at peace only if we allow ourselves to be reconciled, in the Lord Jesus, with the Father and with the brethren. And we have all felt this in our hearts, when we have gone to Confession with a soul weighed down and with a little sadness; and when we receive Jesus' forgiveness we feel at peace, with that peace of soul which is so beautiful, and which only Jesus can give, only him.

Over time, the celebration of this sacrament has passed from a public form — because at first it was made publicly — to a personal one, to the confidential form of Confession. This, however, does not entail losing the ecclesial matrix that constitutes its vital context. In fact, the Christian community is the place where the Spirit is made present, who renews hearts in the love of God and makes all of the brethren one thing in Christ Jesus. That is why it is not enough to ask the Lord for forgiveness in one's own mind and heart, but why instead it is necessary humbly and trustingly to confess one's sins to a minister of the Church. In the celebration of this sacrament, the priest represents not only God but also the whole community, who sees itself in the weakness of each of its members, who listens and is moved by his repentance, and who is reconciled with him, which cheers him up and accompanies him on the path of conversion and human and Christian growth.

One might say: I confess only to God. Yes, you can say to God "forgive me" and say your sins, but our sins are also committed against the brethren, and against the Church. That is why it is necessary to ask pardon of the Church, and of the brethren in the person of the priest. "But Father, I am ashamed...." Shame is also good, it is healthy to feel a little shame, because being ashamed is salutary. In my country when a person feels no shame, we say that he is "shameless"; a "*sin verguenza.*" But shame too does good, because it makes us more humble, and the priest receives this confession with love and tenderness and forgives us on God's behalf. Also from a human point of view, in order to unburden oneself, it is good to talk with a brother and tell the priest these things which are weighing so much on my heart. And one feels that one is unburdening oneself before God, with the Church, with his brother. Do not be afraid of Confession! When one is in line to go to Confession, one feels all these things, even shame, but then when one finishes Confession one leaves free, grand, beautiful, forgiven, candid, happy. This is the beauty of Confession!

I would like to ask you — but don't say it aloud, everyone respond in his heart: when was the last time you made your confession? Everyone think about it.... Two days, two weeks, two years, twenty years, forty years? Everyone count, everyone say, "When was the last time I went

The Church offers all the possibility of following a path of holiness, that is the path of the Christian: she brings us to encounter Jesus Christ in the Sacraments, especially in Confession and in the Eucharist; she communicates the Word of God to us; she lets us live in charity, in the love of God for all. Let us ask ourselves then, will we let ourselves be sanctified? Are we a Church that calls and welcomes sinners with open arms, that gives courage and hope, or are we a Church closed in on herself? Are we a Church where the love of God dwells, where one cares for the other, where one prays for the others?

—— *Pope Francis, General Audience, October 2, 2013*

to Confession?" And if much time has passed, do not lose another day. Go. The priest will be good. Jesus is there, and Jesus is more benevolent than priests, Jesus receives you, he receives you with so much love. Be courageous and go to Confession!

Dear friends, celebrating the sacrament of Reconciliation means being enfolded in a warm embrace: it is the embrace of the Father's infinite mercy. Let us recall that beautiful, beautiful parable of the son who left his home with the money of his inheritance. He wasted all the money and then, when he had nothing left, he decided to return home, not as a son but as a servant. His heart was filled with so much guilt and shame. The surprise came when he began to speak, to ask for forgiveness; his father did not let him speak, he embraced him, he kissed him, and he began to make merry. But I am telling you: each time we go to Confession, God embraces us. God rejoices! Let us go forward on this road. May God bless you!

Chapter 19[1]

The Grace of Being Ashamed

Pope Francis preached about the sacrament of Confession. Commenting on the first Reading of the day, taken from St. Paul's Letter to the Romans (7:18–25), he began by noting that although Paul had experienced the freedom and recreation in Christ's blood, yet he acknowledges that sin still dwells in him, seeking to pull him back into slavery.

Quoting St. Paul, he continued: "I know that nothing good dwells within me, that is, in my flesh. I can will what is right, but I cannot do it. For I do not do the good I want, but the evil I do not want is what I do. Now if I do what I do not want, it is no longer I that do it, but sin which dwells within me."

Pope Francis called this "the Christian battle." Paul speaks of it in this way: "When I want to do the good, evil is right beside me. In fact, I delight in the law of God, in my inmost self, but I see in my members another law at war with the law of the mind, making me captive to the law of sin which dwells in my members." However, the Pope noted, "we do not always have the courage to speak about this battle as Paul does. We always seek to justify ourselves."

---

1   Pope Francis, Meditation in the Chapel of the Domus St. Martha, October 25, 2013, as reported by *L'Osservatore Romano*, Weekly Edition in English, n. 44, November 1, 2013.

It is against this attitude that we must battle. "If we fail to recognize this, we cannot obtain God's forgiveness; if being a sinner is only a word or a way of speaking, then we do not need God's forgiveness. But if it is a reality that enslaves us, then we truly need the interior freedom and strength of the Lord."

Paul shows us the way out, the Pope said. "Confess your sin and your tendency to sin to the community, do not hide it. This is the disposition which the Church asks of all of us, which Jesus asks of all of us: humbly to confess our sins."

The Church in her wisdom points to the sacrament of Confession. "Let us go to our brother the priest and let us make this interior confession, the same confession that Paul himself makes."

The Pontiff then commented on those who refuse to speak with a priest under the pretense that they confess

"We too need to be continually purified through prayer, penance, and through the Sacraments of Reconciliation and the Eucharist," the Holy Father added. Thus "in these two temples — the physical temple which is a place of adoration, and the spiritual temple within me where the Holy Spirit dwells — our disposition should be one of true piety that adores and listens, that prays and asks pardon, that praises the Lord." The Pope then added: "When we speak of the joy of the temple, what we are speaking about is this: the whole community in adoration, in prayer and thanksgiving, in praise. In prayer with the Lord who is within me, since I am a temple; while I stand listening, ready and available."

— *Pope Francis, Meditation in the Chapel of the Domus St. Martha, November 22, 2013, as reported by* L'Osservatore Romano, *Weekly Edition in English, n. 48, November 29, 2013* directly to God. "It's easy," he said. "It's like confessing by email…. God is there, far away; I say things and there is no face to face, there is not a face to face encounter." But Paul "confessed his weakness to his brothers face to face."

Citing the Gospel canticle, Pope Francis confided that he admires the way children make their confession. "During the Alleluia we said: 'I thank thee, Father, Lord of heaven and earth, that thou hast hidden the mysteries of the kingdom from the wise and understanding and revealed them to babes.'" He then added, "Little ones have a certain wisdom. When a child comes to make his confession, he never speaks in generalities. He says: 'Father, I did this, and I did this to my aunt, I did this to someone else, and to someone else I said this word,' and they say the word. They are real, they possess the simplicity of truth. And we always tend to hide the reality of our weakness and poverty."

He then added: "But if there is one thing that is beautiful, it is when we confess our sins in the presence of God just as they are. We always feel the grace of being ashamed. To feel ashamed before God is a grace. It is a grace to say: 'I am ashamed.' Let us think about St. Peter after Jesus' miracle on the lake: 'Depart from me Lord, for I am a sinner.' He was ashamed of his sin."

Going to Confession, the Pope said, is "going to an encounter with the Lord who forgives us, who loves us. And our shame is what we offer him: 'Lord, I am a sinner, but I am not so bad, I am capable of feeling ashamed.'"

The Holy Father concluded: "Let us ask for the grace to live in the truth without hiding anything from the Lord and without hiding anything from ourselves."

Chapter 20[1]

GRACES OF THE ANOINTING
OF THE SICK

I now would like to talk about the sacrament of the Anointing of the Sick, which allows us to touch God's compassion for man. In the past it was called "Extreme Unction," because it was understood as a spiritual comfort in the face of imminent death. To speak instead of the "Anointing of the Sick" helps us broaden our vision to include the experience of illness and suffering, within the horizon of God's mercy.

There is a biblical icon that expresses, in all its depths, the mystery that shines through the Anointing of the Sick: it is the parable of the "Good Samaritan" contained in the Gospel of Luke (10:30–35). Each time we celebrate this sacrament, the Lord Jesus, in the person of the priest, comes close to the one who suffers and is seriously ill or elderly. The parable says that the Good Samaritan takes care of the suffering man by pouring oil and wine on his wounds.

Oil makes us think of that which is blessed by the Bishop each year at the Holy Thursday Chrism Mass, precisely in view of the Anointing of the Sick. Wine, however, is a sign of Christ's love and grace, which flow from the gift of his life for us and are expressed in all their richness in the sacramental life of the Church. Finally, the suffering

---

1   Pope Francis, General Audience, February 26, 2014.

person is entrusted to an innkeeper, so that he might continue to care for him, sparing no expense. Now, who is this innkeeper? It is the Church, the Christian community — it is us — to whom each day the Lord entrusts those who are afflicted in body and spirit, so that we might lavish all of his mercy and salvation upon them without measure.

This mandate is repeated in an explicit and precise manner in the Letter of James, where he recommends: "Is any among you sick? Let him call for the elders of the church, and let them pray over him, anointing him with oil in the name of the Lord; and the prayer of faith will save the sick man, and the Lord will raise him up; and if he has committed sins, he will be forgiven" (5:14–15). It was therefore a practice that was already taking place at the time of the Apostles. Jesus in fact taught his disciples to have the same preferential love that he did for the sick and suffering, and he transmitted to them the ability and duty to continue providing, in his name and after his own heart, relief and peace through the special grace of this sacrament. This, however, should not make us fall into an obsessive search for miracles or the presumption that one can always and in any situation be healed. Rather, it is the reassurance of Jesus' closeness to the sick — and the aged, too — because any elderly person, anyone over the age of 65, can receive this sacrament, through which Jesus himself draws close to us.

But when someone is sick, we at times think: "Let's call for the priest to come"; "No, then he will bring bad luck, let's not call him," or "He will scare the sick person." Why do we think this? Because the idea is floating about that the undertakers arrive after the priest. And this is not true. The priest comes to help the sick or elderly person; that is why the priest's visit to the sick is so important. We ought to call the priest to the sick person's side and say: "Come, give him the anointing, bless him." It is Jesus himself who comes to relieve the sick person, to give him strength, to give him hope, to help him; and also to forgive his sins. And this is very beautiful! And one must not think that this is taboo, because in times of pain and illness it is always good to know that we are not alone: the priest and those who are present during the Anointing of the Sick, in fact, represent the entire Christian community that as one body huddles around the one who suffers and his family, nurturing their faith and hope, and supporting them through their prayers and fraternal warmth.

The greatest comfort comes from the fact that it is the Lord Jesus himself who makes himself present in the sacra-

In a word, a good mother helps her children to come of themselves, and not to remain comfortably under her motherly wings, like a brood of chicks under the wings of the broody hen. The Church, like a good mother, does the same thing: she accompanies our development by transmitting to us the Word of God, which is a light that directs the path of Christian life; she administers the Sacraments. She nourishes us with the Eucharist, she brings us the forgiveness of God through the Sacrament of Penance, she helps us in moments of sickness with the Anointing of the sick. The Church accompanies us throughout our entire life of faith, throughout the whole of our Christian life.

— *Pope Francis, General Audience, September 11, 2013*

ment, who takes us by the hand, who caresses us as he did with the sick, and who reminds us that we already belong to him and that nothing — not even evil and death — can ever separate us from him. Are we in the habit of calling for the priest so that he might come to our sick — I am not speaking about those who are sick with the flu, for three or four days, but rather about a serious illness — and our elderly, and give them this sacrament, this comfort, this strength of Jesus to continue on? Let us do so!

Chapter 21[1]

THE CHURCH AS A FIELD HOSPITAL

I see clearly that the thing the church needs most today is the ability to heal wounds and to warm the hearts of the faithful; it needs nearness, proximity. I see the church as a field hospital after battle. It is useless to ask a seriously injured person if he has high cholesterol and about the level of his blood sugar! You have to heal his wounds. Then we can talk about everything else. Heal the wounds, heal the wounds.... And you have to start from the ground up.

The church sometimes has locked itself up in small things, in small-minded rules. The most important thing is the first proclamation: Jesus Christ has saved you. And the ministers of the church must be ministers of mercy above all. The confessor, for example, is always in danger of being either too much of a rigorist or too lax. Neither is merciful, because neither of them really takes responsibility for the person. The rigorist washes his hands so that he leaves it to the commandment. The loose minister washes his hands by simply saying, "This is not a sin," or something like that. In pastoral ministry we must accompany people, and we must heal their wounds.

How are we treating the people of God? I dream of a church that is a mother and shepherdess. The church's min-

---

1   *America* magazine interview by Antonio Spadaro, S.J., September 30, 2013.

isters must be merciful, take responsibility for the people and accompany them like the good Samaritan, who washes, cleans, and raises up his neighbor. This is pure Gospel. God is greater than sin. The structural and organizational reforms are secondary — that is, they come afterward. The first reform must be the attitude. The ministers of the Gospel must be people who can warm the hearts of the people, who walk through the dark night with them, who know how to dialogue and to descend themselves into their people's night, into the darkness, but without getting lost. The people of God want pastors, not clergy acting like bureaucrats or government officials. The bishops, particularly, must be able to support the movements of God among their people with patience, so that no one is left behind. But they must also be able to accompany the flock that has a flair for finding new paths.

Instead of being just a church that welcomes and receives by keeping the doors open, let us try also to be a church that finds new roads, that is able to step outside itself and go to those who do not attend Mass, to those who have quit or are indifferent. The ones who quit sometimes do it for reasons that, if properly understood and assessed, can lead to a return. But that takes audacity and courage.

Chapter 22[1]

Sacraments of Vocations

We have already had occasion to point out that the three sacraments of Baptism, Confirmation, and the Eucharist together constitute the mystery of "Christian initiation," a single great event of grace that regenerates us in Christ. This is the fundamental vocation that unites everyone in the Church as disciples of the Lord Jesus. There are then two sacraments that correspond to two specific vocations: Holy Orders and Matrimony. They constitute two great paths by which the Christian can make his life a gift of love, after the example and in the name of Christ, and thus cooperate in the building up of the Church.

Holy Orders, in its three grades of bishop, priest, and deacon, is the sacrament that enables a man to exercise the ministry that the Lord Jesus entrusted to the Apostles, to shepherd his flock, in the power of his Spirit and according to his Heart. Tending Jesus' flock not by the power of human strength nor by one's own power, but by the Spirit's and according to his Heart, the Heart of Jesus, which is a heart of love. The priest, the bishop, the deacon must shepherd the Lord's flock with love. It is useless if it is not done with love. And in this sense, the ministers who are chosen and consecrated for this service extend Jesus' presence in

1   Pope Francis, General Audience, March 26, 2014.

time, if they do so by the power of the Holy Spirit, in God's name and with love.

A first aspect. Those who are ordained are placed *at the head of the community*. They are "at the head," yes, but for Jesus this means placing one's authority *at the service* [of the community], as Jesus himself showed and taught his disciples with these words: "You know that the rulers of the Gentiles lord it over them, and their great men exercise authority over them. It shall not be so among you; but whoever would be great among you must be your servant, and whoever would be first among you must be your slave; even as the Son of man came not to be served but to serve, and to give his life as a ransom for many" (Mt 20:25–28/Mk 10:42–45). A bishop who is not at the service of the community fails to perform his duty; a priest who is not at the service of his community fails to perform his duty, he errs.

Another characteristic that also derives from this sacramental union with Christ is a *passionate love for the Church*. Let us think of that passage from the Letter to the Ephesians in which St. Paul states that Christ "loved the Church and gave himself up for her, that he might sanctify her, having cleansed her by the washing of water with the word, that he might present the Church to himself in splendor, without spot or wrinkle or any such thing" (5:25–27). Through Holy Orders the minister dedicates himself entirely to his community and loves it with all his heart: it is his family. The bishop and the priest love the Church in their own community, they love it greatly. How? As Christ loves the Church. St. Paul will say the same of marriage: the husband is to love his wife as Christ loves the Church. It is a great mystery of love: this of priestly ministry and that of matrimony are two sacraments, pathways which people normally take to go to the Lord.

A final aspect. The Apostle Paul recommends to the disciple Timothy that he not neglect, indeed, that *he always rekindle the gift that is within him*. The gift that he has been given through the laying on of hands (cf. 1 Tim 4:14; 2 Tim 1:6). When the ministry is not fostered — the ministry of the bishop, the ministry of the priest — through prayer, through listening to the Word of God, through the daily celebration of the Eucharist, and also through regularly going to the sacrament of Penance, he inevitably ends up losing sight of the authentic meaning of his own service and the joy that comes from a profound communion with Jesus.

The bishop who does not pray, the bishop who does not listen to the Word of God, who does not celebrate every day, who does not regularly confess — and the same is true for the priest who does not do these things — in the long run loses his union with Jesus and becomes so mediocre that he does not benefit the Church. That is why we must help bishops and priests to pray, to listen to the Word of God, which is one's daily nourishment, to celebrate the Eucharist each day, and to confess regularly. This is so important precisely because it concerns the sanctification of bishops and priests.

I would like to conclude with something that comes to mind: how does one become a priest, where is access to the priesthood sold? No; it is not sold. This is an initiative that the Lord takes. The Lord calls. He calls each of those whom he wills to become priests. Perhaps there are some young men present here who have heard this call in their hearts, the aspiration to become a priest, the desire to serve others in the things of God, the desire to spend one's entire life in service in order to catechize, baptize, forgive, celebrate the Eucharist, heal the sick … the whole of one's life in this way. If some of you have heard this call in your heart, it is Jesus who has placed it there. Pay attention to this invitation and pray that it might grow and bear fruit for the whole Church.

Chapter 23[1]

PRIESTLY ORDINATIONS

Beloved brothers and sisters: because these our sons, who are your relatives and friends, are now to be advanced to the Order of priests, consider carefully the nature of the rank in the Church to which they are about to be raised.

It is true that God has made his entire holy people a royal priesthood in Christ. Nevertheless, our great Priest himself, Jesus Christ, chose certain disciples to carry out publicly in his name, and on behalf of mankind, a priestly office in the Church. For Christ was sent by the Father and he in turn sent the Apostles into the world, so that through them and their successors, the Bishops, he might continue to exercise his office of Teacher, Priest, and Shepherd. Indeed, priests are established coworkers of the Order of Bishops, with whom they are joined in the priestly office and with whom they are called to the service of the people of God.

After mature deliberation and prayer, these, our brothers, are now to be ordained to the priesthood in the Order of the presbyterate so as to serve Christ the Teacher, Priest, and Shepherd, by whose ministry his body, that is, the Church, is built and grows into the people of God, a holy temple.

---

1   Pope Francis, Homily, April 21, 2013.

In being configured to Christ the eternal High Priest
and joined to the priesthood of the Bishops, they will be
consecrated as true priests of the New Testament, to preach
the Gospel, to shepherd God's people, and to celebrate the
sacred Liturgy, especially the Lord's sacrifice.

Now, my dear brothers and sons, you are to be raised
to the Order of the Priesthood. For your part you will
exercise the sacred duty of teaching in the name of Christ
the Teacher. Impart to everyone the word of God which
you have received with joy. Remember your mothers,
your grandmothers, your catechists, who gave you the
word of God, the faith … the gift of faith! They transmitted to you this gift of faith. Meditating on the law of the
Lord, see that you believe what you read, that you teach
what you believe, and that you practice what you teach.
Remember too that the word of God is not your property:
it is the word of God. And the Church is the custodian of
the word of God.

In this way, let what you teach be nourishment for the
people of God. Let the holiness of your lives be a delightful
fragrance to Christ's faithful, so that by word and example
you may build up the house which is God's Church.

Likewise you will exercise in Christ the office of sanctifying. For by your ministry the spiritual sacrifice of the
faithful will be made perfect, being united to the sacrifice
of Christ, which will be offered through your hands in an
unbloody way on the altar, in union with the faithful, in
the celebration of the sacraments. Understand, therefore,
what you do and imitate what you celebrate. As celebrants
of the mystery of the Lord's death and resurrection, strive

to put to death whatever in your members is sinful and to walk in newness of life.

You will gather others into the people of God through Baptism, and you will forgive sins in the name of Christ and the Church in the sacrament of Penance. Today I ask you in the name of Christ and the Church, never tire of being merciful. You will comfort the sick and the elderly with holy oil: do not hesitate to show tenderness toward the elderly. When you celebrate the sacred rites, when you offer prayers of praise and thanks to God throughout the hours of the day, not only for the people of God but for the world — remember then that you are taken from among men and appointed on their behalf for those things that pertain to God. Therefore, carry out the ministry of Christ the Priest with constant joy and genuine love, attending not to your own concerns but to those of Jesus Christ. You are pastors, not functionaries. Be mediators, not intermediaries.

Finally, dear sons, exercising for your part the office of Christ, Head and Shepherd, while united with the Bishop and subject to him, strive to bring the faithful together into one family, so that you may lead them to God the Father through Christ in the Holy Spirit. Keep always before your eyes the example of the Good Shepherd who came not to be served but to serve, and who came to seek out and save what was lost.

(The homily delivered by the Holy Father is based on the one that appears in the Pontificale Romanum *for the ordination of priests, with one or two personal additions.)*

Chapter 24[1]

ANOINTED WITH THE OIL
OF GLADNESS

*D**ear Brother Priests*, in the eternal "today" of Holy Thursday, when Christ showed his love for us to the end (cf. Jn 13:1), we recall the happy day of the institution of the priesthood, as well as the day of our own priestly ordination. The Lord anointed us in Christ with the oil of gladness, and this anointing invites us to accept and appreciate this great gift: the gladness, the joy of being a priest. Priestly joy is a priceless treasure, not only for the priest himself but for the entire faithful people of God: that faithful people from which he is called to be anointed and which he, in turn, is sent to anoint.

Anointed with the oil of gladness so as to anoint others with the oil of gladness. Priestly joy has its source in the Father's love, and the Lord wishes the joy of this Love to be "ours" and to be "complete" (cf. Jn 15:11). I like to reflect on joy by contemplating Our Lady, for Mary, the "Mother of the living Gospel, is a wellspring of joy for God's little ones" (*Evangelii Gaudium*, 288). I do not think it is an exaggeration to say that the priest is very little indeed: the incomparable grandeur of the gift granted us for the ministry sets us among the least of men. The priest is the poorest of men unless Jesus enriches him by his poverty, the most

---

1   Pope Francis, Homily, Holy Chrism Mass, April 17, 2014.

useless of servants unless Jesus calls him his friend, the most
ignorant of men unless Jesus patiently teaches him as he
did Peter, the frailest of Christians unless the Good Shepherd strengthens him in the midst of the flock. No one is
more "little" than a priest left to his own devices; and so
our prayer of protection against every snare of the Evil One
is the prayer of our Mother: I am a priest because he has
regarded my littleness (cf. Lk 1:48). And in that littleness
we find our joy. Joy in our littleness!

For me, there are three significant features of our
priestly joy. It is a joy that *anoints us* (not one that "greases"
us, making us unctuous, sumptuous, and presumptuous),
it is a joy that is *imperishable*, and it is a *missionary* joy that
spreads and attracts, starting backwards — with those far-
thest away from us.

A joy that anoints us. In a word: it has penetrated deep
within our hearts, it has shaped them and strengthened
them sacramentally. The signs of the ordination liturgy
speak to us of the Church's maternal desire to pass on and
share with others all that the Lord has given us: the laying
on of hands, the anointing with sacred chrism, the clothing
with sacred vestments, the first consecration that immediately follows.... Grace fills us to the brim and overflows,
fully, abundantly, and entirely in each priest. We are anointed down to our very bones ... and our joy, which wells up
from deep within, is the echo of this anointing.

An imperishable joy. The fullness of the Gift, which
no one can take away or increase, is an unfailing source
of joy: an imperishable joy which the Lord has promised
no one can take from us (Jn 16:22). It can lie dormant,

or be clogged by sin or by life's troubles, yet deep down it remains intact, like the embers of a burnt log beneath the ashes, and it can always be renewed. Paul's exhortation to Timothy remains ever timely: I remind you to fan into flame the gift of God that is within you through the laying on of my hands (cf. 2 Tim 1:6).

A missionary joy. I would like especially to share with you and to stress this third feature: priestly joy is deeply bound up with God's holy and faithful people, for it is an eminently missionary joy. Our anointing is meant for anointing God's holy and faithful people: for baptizing and confirming them, healing and sanctifying them, blessing, comforting, and evangelizing them.

And since this joy is one that only springs up when the shepherd is in the midst of his flock (for even in the silence of his prayer, the shepherd who worships the Father is with his sheep), it is a "guarded joy," watched over by the flock itself. Even in those gloomy moments when everything looks dark and a feeling of isolation takes hold of us, in those moments of listlessness and boredom which at times overcome us in our priestly life (and which I too have experienced), even in those moments God's people are able to "guard" that joy; they are able to protect you, to embrace you, and to help you open your heart to find renewed joy.

A "guarded joy": one guarded by the flock but also guarded by three sisters who surround it, tend it, and defend it: sister poverty, sister fidelity, and sister obedience.

The joy of priests is a joy that is sister to poverty. The priest is poor in terms of purely human joy. He has given up so much! And because he is poor, he, who gives so

much to others, has to seek his joy from the Lord and from
God's faithful people. He doesn't need to try to create it
for himself. We know that our people are very generous in
thanking priests for their slightest blessing and especially
for the sacraments. Many people, in speaking of the crisis
of priestly identity, fail to realize that identity presupposes
belonging. There is no identity — and consequently joy of
life — without an active and unwavering sense of belonging to God's faithful people (cf. *Evangelii Gaudium*, 268).
The priest who tries to find his priestly identity by soul-
searching and introspection may well encounter nothing
more than "exit" signs, signs that say: exit from yourself,
exit to seek God in adoration, go out and give your people
what was entrusted to you, for your people will make you
feel and taste who you are, what your name is, what your
identity is, and they will make you rejoice in that hundred-
fold which the Lord has promised to those who serve him.
Unless you "exit" from yourself, the oil grows rancid and
the anointing cannot be fruitful. Going out from ourselves
presupposes self-denial; it means poverty.

Priestly joy is a joy that is sister to fidelity. Not primarily in the sense that we are all "immaculate" (would that
by God's grace we were!), for we are sinners, but in the
sense of an ever renewed fidelity to the one Bride, to the
Church. Here fruitfulness is key. The spiritual children that
the Lord gives each priest, the children he has baptized, the
families he has blessed and helped on their way, the sick he
has comforted, the young people he catechizes and helps to
grow, the poor he assists ... all these are the "Bride" whom
he rejoices to treat as his supreme and only love and to

whom he is constantly faithful. It is the living Church, with a first name and a last name, which the priest shepherds in his parish or in the mission entrusted to him. That mission brings him joy whenever he is faithful to it, whenever he does all that he has to do and lets go of everything that he has to let go of, as long as he stands firm amid the flock that the Lord has entrusted to him: Feed my sheep (cf. Jn 21:16,17).

Priestly joy is a joy that is sister to obedience. An obedience to the Church in the hierarchy that gives us, as it were, not simply the external framework for our obedience: the parish to which I am sent, my ministerial assignments, my particular work ... but also union with God the Father, the source of all fatherhood. It is likewise an obedience to the Church in service: in availability and readiness to serve everyone, always and as best I can, following the example of "Our Lady of Promptness" (cf. Lk 1:39, *meta spoudes*), who hastens to serve Elizabeth her kinswoman and is concerned for the kitchen of Cana when the wine runs out. The availability of her priests makes the Church a house with open doors, a refuge for sinners, a home for people living on the streets, a place of loving care for the sick, a camp for the young, a classroom for catechizing children about to make their First Communion.... Wherever God's people have desires or needs, there is the priest, who knows how to listen (*ob-audire*) and feels a loving mandate from Christ who sends him to relieve that need with mercy or to encourage those good desires with resourceful charity.

All who are called should know that genuine and complete joy does exist in this world: it is the joy of being taken from the people we love and then being sent back to them as dispensers of the gifts and counsels of Jesus, the one Good Shepherd who, with deep compassion for all the little ones and the outcasts of this earth, wearied and oppressed like sheep without a shepherd, wants to associate many others to his ministry, so as himself to remain with us and to work, in the person of his priests, for the good of his people.

On this Holy Thursday, I ask the Lord Jesus to enable many young people to discover that burning zeal that joy kindles in our hearts as soon as we have the stroke of boldness needed to respond willingly to his call.

On this Holy Thursday, I ask the Lord Jesus to preserve the joy sparkling in the eyes of the recently ordained who go forth to devour the world, to spend themselves fully in the midst of God's faithful people, rejoicing as they prepare their first homily, their first Mass, their first Baptism, their first Confession.... It is the joy of being able to share with wonder, and for the first time as God's anointed, the treasure of the Gospel and to feel the faithful people anointing you again and in yet another way: by their requests, by bowing their heads for your blessing, by taking your hands, by bringing you their children, by pleading for their sick.... Preserve, Lord, in your young priests the joy of going forth, of doing everything as if for the first time, the joy of spending their lives fully for you.

On this Thursday of the priesthood, I ask the Lord Jesus to confirm the priestly joy of those who have already ministered for some years. The joy which, without leaving their eyes, is also found on the shoulders of those who bear the burden of the ministry, those priests who, having experienced the labors of the apostolate, gather their strength and rearm themselves: "get a second wind," as the athletes say. Lord, preserve the depth, wisdom, and maturity of the joy felt by these older priests. May they be able to pray with Nehemiah: "The joy of the LORD is [my] strength" (cf. Neh 8:10).

Finally, on this Thursday of the priesthood, I ask the Lord Jesus to make better known the joy of elderly priests, whether healthy or infirm. It is the joy of the Cross, which springs from the knowledge that we possess an imperishable treasure in perishable earthen vessels. May these priests find happiness wherever they are; may they experience already, in the passage of the years, a taste of eternity (Guardini). May they know, Lord, the joy of handing on the torch, the joy of seeing new generations of their spiritual children, and of hailing the promises from afar, smiling and at peace, in that hope which does not disappoint.

Chapter 25[1]

Anointed Ones

This morning I have the joy of celebrating my first Chrism Mass as the Bishop of Rome. I greet all of you with affection, especially you, dear priests, who, like myself, today recall the day of your ordination.

The readings and the Psalm of our Mass speak of God's "anointed ones": the suffering Servant of Isaiah, King David, and Jesus our Lord. All three have this in common: the anointing that they receive is meant in turn to anoint God's faithful people, whose servants they are; they are anointed for the poor, for prisoners, for the oppressed.... A fine image of this "being for" others can be found in the Psalm 133: "It is like the precious oil upon the head, running down upon the beard, upon the beard of Aaron, running down on the collar of his robes" (v. 2). The image of spreading oil, flowing down from the beard of Aaron upon the collar of his sacred robe, is an image of the priestly anointing that through Christ, the Anointed One, reaches the ends of the earth, represented by the robe.

The sacred robes of the High Priest are rich in symbolism. One such symbol is that the names of the children of Israel were engraved on the onyx stones mounted on the shoulder-pieces of the ephod, the ancestor of our present-day chasuble: six on the stone of the right shoulder-piece

---

1   Pope Francis, Homily, Holy Chrism Mass, March 28, 2013.

and six on that of the left (cf. Ex 28:6–14). The names of the twelve tribes of Israel were also engraved on the breast-plate (cf. Es 28:21). This means that the priest celebrates by carrying on his shoulders the people entrusted to his care and bearing their names written in his heart. When we put on our simple chasuble, it might well make us feel, upon our shoulders and in our hearts, the burdens and the faces of our faithful people, our saints and martyrs who are numerous in these times.

From the beauty of all these liturgical things, which is not so much about trappings and fine fabrics than about the glory of our God resplendent in his people, alive and strengthened, we turn now to a consideration of activity, action. The precious oil that anoints the head of Aaron does more than simply lend fragrance to his person; it over-flows down to "the edges." The Lord will say this clearly: his anointing is meant for the poor, prisoners, and the sick, for those who are sorrowing and alone. My dear brothers, the ointment is not intended just to make us fragrant, much less to be kept in a jar, for then it would become rancid … and the heart bitter.

A good priest can be recognized by the way his people are anointed: this is a clear proof. When our people are anointed with the oil of gladness, it is obvious: for example, when they leave Mass looking as if they have heard good news. Our people like to hear the Gospel preached with "unction," they like it when the Gospel we preach touches their daily lives, when it runs down like the oil of Aaron to the edges of reality, when it brings light to moments of ex-treme darkness, to the "outskirts" where people of faith are most exposed to the onslaught of those who want to tear down their faith. People thank us because they feel that we have prayed over the realities of their everyday lives, their troubles, their joys, their burdens, and their hopes. And when they feel that the fragrance of the Anointed One, of Christ, has come to them through us, they feel encouraged to entrust to us everything they want to bring before the Lord: "Pray for me, Father, because I have this problem," "Bless me, Father," "Pray for me" — these words are the sign that the anointing has flowed down to the edges of the robe, for it has turned into a prayer of supplication, the supplication of the People of God. When we have this relationship with God and with his people, and grace passes through us, then we are priests, mediators between God and men. What I want to emphasize is that we need constantly to stir up God's grace and perceive in every request, even those requests that are inconvenient and at times purely material or downright banal — but only apparently so — the desire of our people to be anointed with fragrant oil, since they know that we have it. To perceive and to sense, even as the Lord sensed the hope-filled anguish of the woman suffering from hemorrhages when she touched the hem of his garment. At that moment, Jesus, surrounded by people on every side, embodies all the beauty of Aaron vested in priestly raiment, with the oil running down upon his robes. It is a hidden beauty, one which shines forth only for those faith-filled eyes of the woman troubled with an issue of blood. But not even the disciples — future priests — see or understand: on the "existential outskirts," they see only what is on the surface: the crowd pressing in on Jesus from all sides (cf. Lk 8:42). The Lord, on the other hand, feels the power of the divine anointing which runs down to the edge of his cloak.

We need to "go out," then, in order to experience our own anointing, its power and its redemptive efficacy: to the "outskirts" where there is suffering, bloodshed, blindness that longs for sight, and prisoners in thrall to many evil masters. It is not in soul-searching or constant introspection that we encounter the Lord: self-help courses can be useful in life, but to live our priestly life going from one course to another, from one method to another, leads us to become pelagians and to minimize the power of grace, which comes alive and flourishes to the extent that we, in faith, go out and give ourselves and the Gospel to others, giving what little ointment we have to those who have nothing, nothing at all.

The priest who seldom goes out of himself, who anoints little — I won't say "not at all" because, thank God, the people take the oil from us anyway — misses out on the best of our people, on what can stir the depths of his priestly heart. Those who do not go out of themselves, instead of being mediators, gradually become intermediaries, managers. We know the difference: the intermediary, the manager, "has already received his reward," and since he doesn't put his own skin and his own heart on the line, he never hears a warm, heartfelt word of thanks. This is precisely the reason for the dissatisfaction of some, who end up sad — sad priests — in some sense becoming collectors of antiques or novelties, instead of being shepherds living with "the odor of the sheep." This I ask you: be shepherds, with the "odor of the sheep," make it real, as shepherds among your flock, fishers of men. True enough, the so-called crisis of priestly identity threatens us all and adds to the broader cultural crisis; but if we can resist its onslaught we will be able to put out in the name of the Lord and cast our nets. It is not a bad thing that reality itself forces us to "put out into the deep," where what we are by grace is clearly seen as pure grace, out into the deep of the contemporary world, where the only thing that counts is "unction" — not function — and the nets which overflow with fish are those cast solely in the name of the One in whom we have put our trust: Jesus.

Dear lay faithful, be close to your priests with affection and with your prayers, that they may always be shepherds according to God's heart.

Dear priests, may God the Father renew in us the Spirit of holiness with whom we have been anointed. May he renew his Spirit in our hearts, that this anointing may spread to everyone, even to those "outskirts" where our faithful people most look for it and most appreciate it. May our people sense that we are the Lord's disciples; may they feel that their names are written upon our priestly vestments and that we seek no other identity; and may they receive through our words and deeds the oil of gladness which Jesus, the Anointed One, came to bring us. Amen.

Chapter 26[1]

MATRIMONY — REFLECTING GOD'S LOVE

We conclude the series of catecheses on the sacraments by speaking about Matrimony. This sacrament leads us to the heart of God's design, which is a plan for a Covenant with his people, with us all — a plan for communion. At the beginning of the book of Genesis, the first book of the Bible, at the culmination of the creation account it says: "God created man in his own image, in the image of God he created him; male and female he created them.... Therefore a man leaves his father and his mother and cleaves to his wife, and they become one flesh" (Gen 1:27; 2:24). The image of God is the married couple: the man and the woman; not only the man, not only the woman, but both of them together. This is the image of God: love, God's covenant with us is represented in that covenant between man and woman. And this is very beautiful! We are created in order to love, as a reflection of God and his love. And in the marital union man and woman fulfil this vocation through their mutual reciprocity and their full and definitive communion of life.

When a man and woman celebrate the sacrament of Matrimony, God as it were "is mirrored" in them; he impresses in them his own features and the indelible character

1 Pope Francis, General Audience, April 2, 2014.

of his love. Marriage is the icon of God's love for us. Indeed, God is communion too: the three Persons of the Father, the Son, and the Holy Spirit live eternally in perfect unity. And this is precisely the mystery of Matrimony: God makes of the two spouses one single life. The Bible uses a powerful expression and says "one flesh," so intimate is the union between man and woman in marriage. And this is precisely the mystery of marriage: the love of God which is reflected in the couple that decides to live together. Therefore a man leaves his home, the home of his parents, and goes to live with his wife and unites himself so strongly to her that the two become — the Bible says — one flesh.

St. Paul, in the Letter to the Ephesians, emphasizes that a great mystery is reflected in Christian spouses: the relationship established by Christ with the Church, a nuptial relationship (cf. Eph 5:21–33). The Church is the bride of Christ. This is their relationship. This means that Matrimony responds to a specific vocation and must be considered as a consecration (cf. *Gaudium et Spes*, n. 48: *Familiaris Consortio*, n. 56). It is a consecration: the man and woman are consecrated in their love. The spouses, in fact, in virtue of the sacrament, are invested with a true and proper mission, so that starting with the simple ordinary things of life they may make visible the love with which Christ loves His Church, by continuing to give his life for her in fidelity and service.

There is a truly marvelous design inherent in the sacrament of Matrimony! And it unfolds in the simplicity and frailty of the human condition. We are well aware of how many difficulties two spouses experience.... The important

Marriage is also an everyday task, I could say a craftsman's task, a goldsmith's work, because the husband has the duty of making the wife more of a woman and the wife has the duty of making the husband more of a man. Growing also in humanity, as man and woman. And this you do together. This is called growing together. This does not come out of thin air! The Lord blesses it but it comes from your hands, from your attitudes, from your way of loving each other. To make us grow! Always act so that the other may grow.

— *Pope Francis, Address to Engaged Couples Preparing for Marriage, February 14, 2014*

thing it to keep alive their bond with God, who stands as the foundation of the marital bond. And the true bond is always the Lord. When the family prays, the bond is preserved. When the husband prays for his wife and the wife prays for her husband, that bond becomes strong; one praying for the other. It is true that there are so many difficulties in married life, so many, when there is insufficient work or money, when the children have problems. So much to contend with. And many times the husband and wife become a little fractious and argue between themselves. They argue, this is how it is, there is always arguing in marriage, sometimes the plates even fly. Yet we must not become saddened by this, this is the human condition. The secret is that love is stronger than the moment when there is arguing, and therefore I always advise spouses: do not let a day when you have argued end without making peace. Always! And to make peace it isn't necessary to call the United Nations to come to the house and make peace. A little gesture is sufficient, a caress, and then let it be! Until tomorrow! And tomorrow begin again. And this is life, carrying on, carrying on with courage and the desire to live together. And this is truly great, it is beautiful! Married life is such a beautiful thing, and we must treasure it always, treasure the children.

On other occasions I have mentioned something else which is so helpful for marriage. There are three words that always need to be said, three words that need to be said at home: may I, thank you, and sorry. The three magic words. *May I*: so as not to be intrusive in the life of the spouses. May I, but how does it seem to you? May I, please allow me. *Thank you*: to thank one's spouse; thank you for what you did for me, thank you for this. That beauty of giving thanks! And since we all make mistakes, that other word which is a bit hard to say but which needs to be said: *sorry*. Please, thank you, and sorry. With these three words, with the prayer of the husband for the wife and vice versa, by always making peace before the day comes to an end, marriage will go forward. The three magic words, prayer, and always making peace. May the Lord bless you; and pray for me.

Chapter 27[1]

THREE LOVES FOR ONE WEDDING

I n his homily at Santa Marta, Pope Francis offered a reflection on love, which came primarily from Jesus' fare-
well address to the Apostles, from today's reading from
the Gospel of John (16:29–33). For fifteen married couples celebrating their wedding anniversaries, this Mass was
a small anniversary party. Taking the experience of these
families as his starting point, the Pope indicated the essential elements of the sacrament of Marriage and "of Jesus'
spousal love for the Church," that is, "for all of us": fidelity,
perseverance, and fruitfulness.

Jesus, Pope Francis explained, "reflected on the same
topic: the world, the spirit of the world, which really hurts
us, and the Spirit that he brings, the Spirit of the Beati-
tudes, the Spirit of the Father." He stated expressly: "The
Father is with me," and for this reason he overcame the
world.

"The Father sent Jesus to us," the Bishop of Rome
stated, because "he loved the world so much that he sent
his Son to save it, out of love." Thus "Jesus was sent out of
love, and Jesus loves." But what is the love of Jesus? The
Pope noted that "many times we read nonsense about the

1   Pope Francis, Meditation in the Chapel of the Domus St. Martha,
June 2, 2014, as reported by *L'Osservatore Romano*, Weekly Edition in
English, n. 23, June 6, 2014.

love of Jesus! But Jesus' love is great." And, in particular, he indicated "three loves of Jesus."

First of all, Jesus "truly loved the Father in the Holy Spirit." It is a "mysterious" and "eternal" love. Such that "we cannot imagine how great, how beautiful this love is"; we can "only ask for the grace to be able to see it once, when we are there." The "second love of Jesus is his Mother." We see him "at the end: in so much pain and with so much suffering, from the Cross he thought of his mother and said, "Take care of her!" Lastly, "the third love of Jesus is the Church, his beloved bride: beautiful, holy, sinful, yet he loves her just the same."

The presence of the fifteen couples inspired the second part of the Pope's meditation. "St. Paul," he explained, "when referring to the sacrament of Marriage, he called it the great sacrament, because Jesus is married to his Church, and every Christian marriage is a reflection of Jesus' marriage to the Church."

The Pope then confided that he would like to ask each couple to tell "what transpired in this time, in these sixty years, fifty years, twenty years." But, he quickly added, "we would not even finish by noon: so we will leave it be!" However, he continued, "we can say something about the spousal love of Jesus for the Church." A love that has "three features: it is faithful; it perseveres — he never tires of loving his Church; and it is fruitful."

Above all, "it is a faithful love." Jesus is the "faithful one," as St. Paul also reminds us. "Fidelity" — said the Pope — "is the very being of Jesus' love. And Jesus' love for his Church is faithful. This fidelity is like a light on the marriage: the fidelity of love, always!" The Pope recognized that "there are hard times, many times you argue. But in the end you return, you ask for forgiveness, and the matrimonial love goes forward, like the love of Jesus for the Church."

Married life, then, is "also a persevering love," because, if this dedication is missing "love cannot go forward." "Perseverance" is necessary "in love, in good times and in difficult times, when there are problems with the children, economic problems." Even in these predicaments "love perseveres, it always moves forward, seeking to resolve things in order to save the family." Once again addressing the couples present, most of all those celebrating sixty years of married life, the Bishop of Rome remarked on the beauty of this experience of perseverance, witnessed by "the man and woman who get up every morning and bring their family forward."

The Pontiff then talked about fertility, "the third trait of Jesus' love for his bride, the Church. The love of Jesus makes his bride fruitful, renders the Church fruitful with new children and baptisms. And the Church grows with this nuptial fruitfulness of Jesus' love." But "sometimes the Lord does not send children: it is a test." And "there are other tests: when a sick child arrives, many problems." And "these tests bring the marriage forward, when they look at Jesus, and take strength from the fruitfulness that Jesus has with his Church, from the love that Jesus has for his Church."

Pope Francis bore in mind "that Jesus does not like marriages in which couples do not want children, in which they want to remain fruitless." They are the product of "the well-off culture of ten years ago," according to which "not having children is better, this way you can travel and see the world, you can have a house in the country and relax!" It is a culture that suggests "it is more comfortable to have a little dog and two cats," this way "love is given to the two cats and the little dog." But living this way "in the end of this marriage old age arrives in solitude, with the bitterness of awful loneliness: it is fruitless, it does not do what Jesus does with his Church."

The Pope concluded with a prayer for the married couples, asking "the Lord that your marriage be beautiful, with crosses to bear but beautiful, like that of Jesus and his Church: faithful, persevering, and fruitful."

Chapter 28[1]

THREE PHRASES FOR MARRIAGE

Living together is an art, a patient, beautiful, fascinating journey. It does not end once you have won each other's love.... Rather, it is precisely there where it begins! This journey of every day has a few rules that can be summed up in three phrases which you already said, phrases which I have already repeated many times to families, and which you have already learned to use among yourselves: *"May I"* — that is, *"can I,"* you said — *"thank you,"* and *"I'm sorry."*

"Can I, may I?" This is the polite request to enter the life of another with respect and care. One should learn how to ask: may I do this? Would you like for us to do this? Should we take up this initiative, to educate our children in this way? Do you want to go out tonight?... In short, to ask permission means to know how to enter with courtesy into the lives of others. Pay attention to this: to know how to enter with courtesy into the lives of others. It's not easy, not easy at all. Sometimes, however, manners are used in a heavy way, like hiking boots! True love does not impose itself harshly and aggressively. In the *Fioretti* of St. Francis we find this expression: "For know, dear brother, that courtesy is one of the attributes of God, for courtesy is the sister of

1   Pope Francis, Address to Engaged Couples Preparing for Marriage, February 14, 2014.

charity, it extinguisheth hatred and kindleth love" (Ch. 37).
Yes, courtesy kindles love. And today in our families, in our
world, which is frequently violent and arrogant, there is so
much need for courtesy. And this can begin at home.

"Thank you." It seems so easy to say these words, but
we know that it is not. But it is important! We teach it
to children, but then we ourselves forget it! Gratitude is
an important sentiment! Do you remember the Gospel of
Luke? An old woman once said to me in Buenos Aires:
"Gratitude is a flower that grows on a noble ground." No-
bility of soul is necessary so that this flower might grow. Do
you remember the Gospel of Luke? Jesus heals ten lepers
and then only one returns to say thank you to Jesus. The
Lord says: and the other nine, where are they? This also
holds true for us: do we know how to give thanks? In your
relationship, and tomorrow in married life, it is important
to keep alive the awareness that the other person is a gift
from God — and for the gifts of God we say thank you! —
we must always give thanks for them. And in this interior
attitude one says thank you to the other for everything. It
is not a kind word to use with strangers, to show you are
polite. You need to know how to say thank you in order to
go forward in a good way together in married life.

The third: *"I'm sorry."* In life we err frequently; we
make many mistakes. We all do. Wait, maybe someone here
has never made a mistake? Raise your hand if you are that
someone, there: a person who has never made a mistake?
We all do it! All of us! Perhaps not a day goes by without
making some mistake. The Bible says that the just man sins
seven times a day. And, thus, we make mistakes.... Hence

the need to use these simple words: "I'm sorry." In general, each of us is ready to accuse the other and to justify ourselves. This began with our father, Adam, when God asks him: "Adam, have you eaten of the fruit?" "Me? No! It was her, she gave it to me!" Accusing the other to avoid saying "I'm sorry," "forgive me." It's an old story! It is an instinct that stands at the origin of so many disasters. Let us learn to acknowledge our mistakes and to ask for forgiveness. "Forgive me if today I raised my voice"; "I'm sorry if I passed without greeting you"; "excuse me if I was late," "if this week I was very silent," "if I spoke too much without ever listening"; "excuse me if I forgot"; "I'm sorry I was angry and I took it out on you." ... We can say many "I'm sorrys" every day. In this way, too, a Christian family grows.

We all know that the perfect family does not exist, nor a perfect husband or wife ... we won't even speak about a perfect mother-in-law. We sinners exist. Jesus, who knows us well, teaches us a secret: don't let a day end without asking forgiveness, without peace returning to our home, to our family. It is normal for husband and wife to quarrel, but there is always something, we had quarreled.... Perhaps you were mad, perhaps plates flew, but please remember this: never let the sun go down without making peace! Never, never, never! This is a secret, a secret for maintaining love and making peace. Pretty words are not necessary.... Sometimes just a simple gesture and ... peace is made. Never let a day end ... for if you let the day end without making peace, the next day what is inside of you is cold and hardened and it is even more difficult to make peace. Remember: never let the sun go down without making peace!

If we learn to say sorry and ask one another for forgiveness, the marriage will last and move forward. When elderly couples, celebrating fifty years together, come to audiences or Mass here at Santa Marta, I ask them: "Who supported whom?" This is beautiful! Everyone looks at each other, they look at me and say: "Both!" And this is beautiful! This is a beautiful witness!

Chapter 29[1]

"Good News" of the Family

The first point which I would like to consider is this: *the family is a community of life which has its own autonomous consistency.* As Blessed John Paul II wrote in the Apostolic Exhortation *Familiaris Consortio*, the family is not merely the sum of persons belonging to it, but a "community of persons" (cf. nn. 17–18). And a community is more than the sum total of persons who belong to it. It is the place where one learns to love, it is the natural center of human life. It is made up of faces, of people who love, dialogue, make self-sacrifices for one another and defend life, especially of the most vulnerable and the weakest. One could say, without exaggeration, that the family is the driving force of the world and of history. Our personality develops in the family, by growing up with our mom and dad, our brothers and sisters, by breathing in the warmth of the home. The family is the place where we receive our name, it is the place of affection, the space of intimacy, where one acquires the art of dialogue and interpersonal communication. In the family the person becomes aware of his or her own dignity and, especially if their upbringing is Christian, each one recognizes the dignity of every single person, in a particular way the sick, the weak, and the marginalized.

---

1   Pope Francis, Address to Participants in the Plenary Assembly of the Pontifical Council for the Family, October 25, 2013.

The family-community is all of this, and it needs to be recognized as such, and more urgently today when the protection of individual rights prevail. And we must defend the right of this community: the family. In this regard you have done well to pay special attention to the *Charter of the Rights of the Family* presented exactly thirty years ago on October 22, 1983.

We come to the second point. They say Jesuits always speak in threes — three points: one, two, three. The second point: *the family is founded on marriage*. Through their free and faithful act of love, Christian spouses testify to the fact that marriage, insofar as it is a sacrament, is the foundation of the family and strengthens spousal union and the couple's mutual gift of self. It is as though matrimony were first a human sacrament, where the person discovers himself, understands himself in relation to others and in a relationship of love which is capable of receiving and giving. Spousal and familial love also clearly reveals the vocation of the person to love in a unique way and forever, and that the trials, sacrifices, and crises of couples as well as of the family as a whole represent pathways for growth in goodness, truth, and beauty. In marriage, we give ourselves completely, without calculation or reserve, sharing everything, gifts and hardship, trusting in God's Providence. This is the experience that the young can learn from their parents and grandparents. It is an experience of faith in God and of mutual trust, profound freedom, and holiness, because holiness presumes giving oneself with fidelity and sacrifice every day of one's life! But there are problems in marriage. Always different points of view, jealousy, arguing. But we need to say to young spouses that they should never end the day without making peace. The sacrament of Marriage is renewed in this act of peace after an argument, a misunderstanding, a hidden jealousy, even a sin. Making peace gives unity to the family; and tell young people, young couples, that it is not easy to go down this path, but it is a very beautiful path, very beautiful. You need to tell them!

Lastly, I would like to mention the two stages of family life: *childhood and old age*. Children and the elderly are the two poles of life and the most vulnerable as well, often the most forgotten. When I hear the confession of a young married man or woman, and in the confessional when some reference is made to a son or a daughter, I ask: but how many children do you have? And they tell me, maybe they expect another question after this one. But this is always my second question: And tell me, Mr. or Mrs., do you play with your children? "Excuse me, Father?" Do you spend time with your children? Do you play with your children? "Well no, you know, when I leave the house in the morning," the man tells me, "they are still asleep and when I come home they are in bed." Availability, the availability of a father or mother to their children, is so important: "spend time" with your children, play with your children. A society that neglects children and marginalizes the elderly severs its roots and darkens its future. And you have been assessing what our culture today is doing, haven't you? Every time a child is abandoned and an elderly person cast out, not only is it an act of injustice, but it also ensures the failure of that society. Caring for our little ones and for our elders is a choice for civilization. And also for the future, because the little ones, the children, the young people will carry society forward by their strength, their youth, and the elderly people will carry it forward by their wisdom, their memory, which they must give to us all.

And it makes me rejoice that the Pontifical Council for the Family has designed this new icon of the family, taking up the image of the Presentation of the Jesus in the Temple with Mary and Joseph carrying the Child in fulfillment of the Law, and the elderly Simeon and Anna who, moved by the Holy Spirit, welcome him as the Savior. The title of the icon is meaningful: *"And His mercy is from generation to generation."* The Church that cares for children and the elderly becomes the mother of generations of believers and, at the same time, serves human society because a spirit of love, familiarity, and solidarity helps all people to rediscover the fatherhood and motherhood of God.

And when I read this Gospel passage I like to think about the fact that those young people, Joseph and Mary, as well as the Child, abide by the Law. Four times St. Luke says: in fulfillment of the Law. They are obedient to the Law, the young people! And the two Elders, they are the ones to make noise! Simeon at that moment invents his own liturgy and praises, he praises God. And the old woman goes and talks, she preaches through her chatter: "Look at him!" They are so free! And three times it states that the Elders are led by the Holy Spirit. The young by the law, the Elders by the Holy Spirit. Look to our elderly people who have this spirit within them, listen to them!

The "Good News" of the family is a very important part of evangelization, which Christians can communicate to all, by the witness of their lives; and already they are doing so, this is evident in secularized societies: truly Christian families are known by their fidelity, their patience, their openness to life, and by their respect for the elderly ... the secret to this is the presence of Jesus in the family. Let us therefore propose to all people, with respect and courage, the beauty of marriage and the family illuminated by the Gospel! And in order to do this let us approach with care and affection those families who are struggling, forced to leave their homeland, broken, homeless or unemployed, or suffering for any reason; let us approach married couples in crisis or separated. Let us be close to everyone through the proclamation of this Gospel of the family, the beauty of the family.

Dear friends, your work during this Plenary can be a valuable contribution to the next Extraordinary Synod of Bishops, which will be dedicated to the family. For this, too, I thank you. I entrust you to the Holy Family of Nazareth and with all my heart I impart my Blessing.

Chapter 30[1]

FORGIVE EACH OTHER

I want to share with you an expression taken from the Rite of Marriage. Those who celebrate the sacrament say, *"I promise to be true to you, in joy and in sadness, in sickness and in health; I will love you and honor you all the days of my life."* At that moment, the couple does not know what will happen, nor what joys and pains await them. They are setting out, like Abraham, on a journey together. And that is what marriage is! Setting out and walking together, hand in hand, putting yourselves in the Lord's powerful hands. Hand in hand, always and for the rest of your lives. And do not pay attention to this makeshift culture, which can shatter our lives.

With trust in God's faithfulness, everything can be faced responsibly and without fear. Christian spouses are not naive; they know life's problems and temptations. But they are not afraid to be responsible before God and before society. They do not run away, they do not hide, they do not shirk the mission of forming a family and bringing children into the world. But today, Father, it is difficult.... Of course it is difficult! That is why we need the grace, the grace that comes from the sacrament! The sacraments are not decorations in life — what a beautiful marriage, what a beautiful ceremony, what a beautiful banquet.... But that is

---

1   Pope Francis, Address to Families, October 26, 2013.

not the sacrament of Marriage. That is a decoration! Grace is not given to decorate life but rather to make us strong in life, giving us courage to go forward! And without isolating oneself but always staying together. Christians celebrate the sacrament of Marriage because they know they need it! They need it to stay together and to carry out their mission as parents. *"In joy and in sadness, in sickness and in health."* This is what the spouses say to one another during the celebration of the sacrament, and in their marriage they pray with one another and with the community. Why? Because it is helpful to do so? No! They do so because they need to, for the long journey they are making together: it is a long journey, not for a brief spell but for an entire life! And they need Jesus' help to walk beside one another in trust, to accept one another each day, and daily to forgive one another. And this is important! To know how to forgive one another in families because we all make mistakes, all of us! Sometimes we do things that are not good and that harm others. It is important to have the courage to ask for forgiveness when we are at fault in the family. Some weeks ago, in this very square, I said that in order to have a healthy family, three words need to be used. And I want to repeat these three words: please, thank you, sorry. Three essential words! We say please so as not to be forceful in family life: "May I please do this? Would you be happy if I did this?" We do this with a language that seeks agreement. We say thank you, thank you for love! But be honest with me, how many times do you say thank you to your wife, and you to your husband? How many days go by without uttering this word, thanks! And the last word: sorry. We all make mistakes and on occasion someone gets offended in the marriage, in the family, and sometimes — I say — plates are smashed, harsh words are spoken, but please listen to my advice: don't ever let the sun set without reconciling. Peace is made each day in the family: "Please forgive me," and then you start over. Please, thank you, sorry! Shall we say them together? [They reply "yes."] Please, thank you, and sorry. Let us say these words in our families! To forgive one another each day!

The life of a family is filled with beautiful moments: rest, meals together, walks in the park or the countryside, visits to grandparents or to a sick person.... But if love is missing, joy is missing, nothing is fun. Jesus gives, always gives us that love: he is its endless source. In the sacrament he gives us his word and he gives us the bread of life, so that our joy may be complete.

Chapter 31[1]

THE BAPTIZED AND THE NEW EVANGELIZATION

In virtue of their baptism, all the members of the People of God have become missionary disciples (cf. Mt 28:19). All the baptized, whatever their position in the Church or their level of instruction in the faith, are agents of evangelization, and it would be insufficient to envisage a plan of evangelization to be carried out by professionals while the rest of the faithful would simply be passive recipients. The new evangelization calls for personal involvement on the part of each of the baptized. Every Christian is challenged, here and now, to be actively engaged in evangelization; indeed, anyone who has truly experienced God's saving love does not need much time or lengthy training to go out and proclaim that love. Every Christian is a missionary to the extent that he or she has encountered the love of God in Christ Jesus: we no longer say that we are "disciples" and "missionaries," but rather that we are always "missionary disciples." If we are not convinced, let us look at those first disciples, who, immediately after encountering the gaze of Jesus, went forth to proclaim him joyfully: "We have found the Messiah!" (Jn 1:41). The Samaritan woman became a missionary immediately after speaking

---

1   Pope Francis, Apostolic Exhortation, *Evangelii Gaudium*, November 24, 2013.

with Jesus and many Samaritans come to believe in him "because of the woman's testimony" (Jn 4:39). So too, St. Paul, after his encounter with Jesus Christ, "immediately ... proclaimed Jesus" (Acts 9:20; cf. 22:6–21). So what are we waiting for?

Chapter 32[1]

THE CHURCH IS OUR MOTHER

Among the images that the Second Vatican Council chose to help us understand the nature of the Church better, there is that of "mother": the Church is our mother in faith, in supernatural life (cf. Dogmatic Constitution, *Lumen Gentium*, nn. 6, 14, 15, 41, 42). It is one of the images most used by the Fathers of the Church in the first centuries and I think it could be useful for us too. For me it is one of the most beautiful images of the Church: Mother Church! In what sense and in what way is the Church mother? We start with the human reality of motherhood: what makes a mother?

First of all a mother generates life, she carries her child in her womb for nine months and then delivers him to life, giving birth to him. The Church is like this: she bears us in the faith, through the work of the Holy Spirit who makes her fertile, like the Virgin Mary. The Church and the Virgin Mary are mothers, both of them; what is said of the Church can be said also of Our Lady and what is said of Our Lady can also be said of the Church! Certainly faith is a personal act: "I believe," I personally respond to God who makes himself known and wants to enter into friendship with me (cf. *Lumen Fidei*, n. 39). But the faith I receive from others, within a family, within a community

1 Pope Francis, General Audience, September 11, 2013.

that teaches me to say "I believe," "we believe." A Christian is not an island! We do not become Christians in a laboratory, we do not become Christians alone and by our own effort, since the faith is a gift, it is a gift from God given to us in the Church and through the Church. And the Church gives us the life of faith in Baptism: that is the moment in which she gives birth to us as children of God, the moment she gives us the life of God, she engenders us as a mother would.

If you go to the Baptistery of St. John Lateran, beside the Pope's Cathedral, inside it there is an inscription in Latin that reads, more or less: "Here is born a people of divine lineage, generated by the Holy Spirit who makes these waters life-giving; Mother Church gives birth to her children within these waves." This makes us understand something important: our taking part in the Church is not an exterior or formal fact, it is not filling out a form they give us; it is an interior and vital act; one does not belong to the Church as one belongs to a society, to a party, or to any other organization. The bond is vital, like the bond you have with your mother, because, as St. Augustine says, "The Church is truly the mother of Christians" (*De moribus Ecclesiae*, I, 30, 62–63: PL 32, 1336). Let us ask ourselves: how do I see the Church? As I am grateful to my parents for giving me life, am I grateful to the Church for generating me in the faith through Baptism?

How many Christians remember the date of their Baptism? I would like to ask you here, but each of you respond in your heart: how many of you remember the date of your Baptism? A few people raise their hands, but many others do not remember! But the date of your Baptism is the day of our birth in the Church, the date on which our mother Church gave us life! And now I leave you with some homework. When you go home today, go and find out what the date of your Baptism is, and then celebrate it, thank the Lord for this gift. Are you going to do it? Do we love the Church as we love our mothers, also taking into account her defects? All mothers have defects. We all have defects. But when we speak of our mother's defects we gloss over them, we love her as she is. And the Church also has her defects: but we love her just as a mother. Do we help her to be more beautiful, more authentic, more in harmony with the Lord? I leave you with these questions, but don't forget your homework: go find the date of your Baptism, carry it in your heart and celebrate it.

Second, a mother does not stop at just giving life; with great care she helps her children grow, gives them milk, feeds them, teaches them the way of life, accompanies them always with her care, with her affection, with her love, even when they are grown up. And in this she also knows to correct them, to forgive them and understand them. She knows how to be close to them in sickness and in suffering. In a word, a good mother helps her children to come of themselves, and not to remain comfortably under her motherly wings, like a brood of chicks under the wings of the broody hen. The Church, like a good mother, does the same thing: she accompanies our development by transmitting to us the Word of God, which is a light that directs the path of Christian life; she administers the sacraments. She nourishes us with the Eucharist, she brings us the forgiveness of God through the sacrament of Penance, she helps us in moments of sickness with the Anointing of the sick. The Church accompanies us throughout our entire life of faith, throughout the whole of our Christian life. We can then ask ourselves other questions: What is my relationship with the Church? Do I feel like she is my mother who helps me grow as a Christian? Do I participate in the life of the Church, do I feel part of it? Is my relationship a formal or a vital relationship?

A third brief thought. In the first centuries of the Church, one thing was very clear: the Church, while being the mother of Christians, while "making" Christians, is also "made" by them. The Church is not distinct from us, but should be seen as the totality of believers, as the "we" of Christians: I, you, we all are part of the Church. St. Jerome wrote: "The Church of Christ is nothing other than the souls of those who believe in Christ" (Tract. Ps 86: PL 26, 1084). Thus the motherhood of the Church is lived by us all, pastors and faithful. At times I feel: "I believe in God but not in the Church.... I have heard that the Church says ... priests say...." Priests are one thing but the church is not formed solely by priests, the Church is all of us! And if you say that you believe in God and you don't believe in the Church, you are saying that you don't believe in yourself; and this is a contradiction. The Church is all of us: from the baby just baptized to the Bishop, the Pope; we are all the Church and we are all equal in the eyes of God! We are all called to collaborate for the birth of new Christians in the faith, we are all called to be educators in the faith, to proclaim the Gospel. Each of us should ask ourselves:

What do I do so that others might share in Christian life? Am I generous in my faith or am I closed? When I repeat that I love a Church that is not closed in herself, but capable of coming out, of moving, even with risks, to bring Christ to all people, I am thinking of everyone, of me, of you, of every Christian! We all take part in the motherhood of the church, so that the light of Christ may reach the far confines of the earth. Long live Holy Mother Church!

More Books by POPE FRANCIS from Our Sunday Visitor

ONLY LOVE CAN SAVE US
LETTERS, HOMILIES, AND TALKS OF
CARDINAL JORGE BERGOGLIO

THROUGH THE YEAR WITH POPE FRANCIS
DAILY REFLECTIONS

NEW BEGINNING, NEW HOPE
HOMILIES OF POPE FRANCIS, HOLY WEEK
THROUGH PENTECOST

A YEAR OF MERCY WITH POPE FRANCIS
DAILY REFLECTIONS

Our Sunday Visitor Publishing
1-800-348-2440
www.osv.com